Reese on Play

Terence Reese

Better Bridge Now

CHESS & BRIDGE LTD

First published in Great Britain in 2001, reprinted 2006.
by Chess & Bridge Limited
369 Euston Road, London NW1 3AR

Distribution:

USA and Canada: Master Point Press
331 Douglas Avenue, Toronto, Ontario, Canada M5M 1H2;
tel: (416) 781 0351; web: www.masterpointpress.com

For all other enquiries, please contact the publishers,
Chess & Bridge Limited, 369 Euston Road, London NW1 3AR;
tel: 020 7388 2404; fax: 020-7388 2407;
email: info@bridgeshop.com; web: bridgemagazine.co.uk

British Library Cataloguing in Publication Data.
A CIP record of this book is available on request from the British Library.

ISBN 0-9530218-2-3

Typeset by
Wakewing Ltd, 73 Totteridge Lane, High Wycombe, Bucks HP13 7QA

Printed in Great Britain by
The Cromwell Press, Trowbridge

Contents

Foreword

When one speaks of bridge writers, the name Terence Reese is synonymous with excellence. Several of his books are landmarks in the development and understanding of bridge, especially in the field of card play. That is especially true of *Reese on Play*, first published more than fifty years ago. This masterpiece explains what counts in play, and introduces the reader to the techniques and strategies that are fundamental to good play and defence.

A measure of the author's genius is that when the deals in this book were checked using the double-dummy analyser Deep Finesse, it revealed only a few minor flaws.

In this revised edition, I have also endeavoured to correct all the typographical errors and eliminated most of the 'x's, replacing them with spot cards.

Including this title in the Better Bridge Now series was an easy decision to make. It instructs and entertains, and will surely inspire you to take another step up the bridge ladder.

Mark Horton
Editor
Better Bridge Now

PART ONE
MAINLY ATTACK

1

What Counts in Play

Good players differ from average players mostly in this: that the good player tries to play all 52 cards, and the average player plays only the 26 which he can see. A player may have first-class technique, but if he plays blind, in the sense that he does not try to reconstruct the unseen hands, he cannot be better than fair; while a player who does this, even if he knows little of elimination and nothing of squeeze play, is a player in a thousand.

To count the opponents' hands requires no special talent. From a defender's side, for example, the distribution of the suit led is often established at the first trick and almost always when the suit is played a second time; then a round or two of trumps by declarer and nine times out of ten it is possible to say how many trumps he started with. So in most cases the distribution of two suits is known after three or four leads; and as a rule the picture can be completed a trick or two later. There is nothing very difficult or abstruse about this kind of analysis; but it does require a conscious effort, and very few players consistently make the effort.

It is not so easy for declarer to gauge the distribution of the defending hands; he has much less to go on, especially in respect of inferences from the bidding. In the early stages of most hands declarer hass to rely on his knowledge of simple probabilities; as the play develops, the picture of the enemy distribution becomes more clear. There is nothing very remarkable about the hand which follows; but it will serve as a starting-point for discussion.

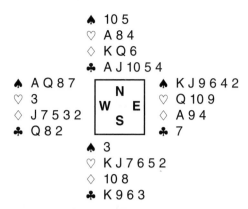

East-West were vulnerable and North dealt. The bidding was:

South	West	North	East
–	–	1♣	1♠
2♡	3♠	4♡	4♠
5♡	All Pass		

The ace of spades was led, followed by another spade, which declarer trumped. The problem was to place the missing queens correctly. Declarer decided that as the opponents had bid to four spades vulnerable, the trumps were more likely to be 3-1 than 2-2. So when East followed to a second trump, South successfully finessed the jack.

This hurdle over, it remained only to find the queen of clubs. As West had a singleton heart, it was likely that he had the long clubs. To complete the count of the hand, South played diamonds before tackling the clubs. After three rounds of diamonds it was established that East held six cards in the red suits; as East had made the overcall of One Spade it was likely that he had six spades, so declarer finessed clubs against West with every confidence.

Only the two aces were lost, so South landed his contract of five hearts. Most players would have done as much, but although the play was not difficult it does raise some important points. First of all, the finesse in trumps before much was known about the East/West hands: there was an inference to be drawn from the bidding that the trumps were more likely to be 3-1 than 2-2, but suppose there had been no opposition bidding: then would it have been right to finesse trumps or to play for the drop?

The answer depends mainly on the simple probabilities. Precise odds can be quoted to show the likely distribution of any number of outstanding cards. The odds are as follows:

The simple probabilities

Two cards will be divided 1-1 52 times in a hundred, 2-0 48 times. Other things being equal, therefore, it is slightly better to play for the drop than to finesse with king and one other card outstanding.

Three cards will be divided 2-1 78 times, 3-0 22 times.

Four cards will be divided 3-1 50 times, 2-2 40 times, 4-0 10 times. But although 3-1 is rather more probable than 2-2, it does not follow from this that when nine cards are held and a queen is missing, it is better to finesse than to play for the drop of the queen. The odds vary every time a card is played; when the moment arrives for declarer to make the decision on the second round of the suit, the odds slightly favour the play for the drop. So when the trump suit was played in the hand above, simple probabilities favoured the play for the drop on the second round rather than the finesse.

Five cards will be divided 3-2 68 times, 4-1 28 times, 5-0 4 times.

Six cards will be divided 4-2 48 times, 3-3 36 times, 5-1 15 times, 6-0 once.

Seven cards will be divided 4-3 62 times, 5-2 31 times, 6-1 7 times, 7-0 less than 0.5 times.

Knowledge of probabilities is of considerable importance in play. For example, a declarer should know that a finesse, which is a 50-50 chance, is a better proposition than the play for the 3-3 split of six outstanding cards, but not so good as the play for a 4-3 split of seven outstanding cards. Of course there are generally clues available which affect normal expectation. For example, one player may be known from the bidding or from the play to have unusual length in one suit. Then naturally his partner is more Likely to have length in another.

There is another factor to be considered. The further the play has advanced, the more likely are the even divisions. For example, if in the middle of the play a declarer with a combined seven cards in a suit plays two rounds, to which all follow, it is better than evens that the two outstanding cards will break 1-1; in other words, a 3-3 break has become more likely than 4-2.

A count to avoid a finesse

We have wandered some way from the original hand, but there is one more point about it which is worth noticing: that is declarer's play of three rounds of diamonds in order to complete his count of the hand. Although in general it is more difficult for declarer to count the hands than it is for a defender, declarer has this advantage, that he can plan the play so as to obtain a complete picture of the hand. He does this on the following deal.

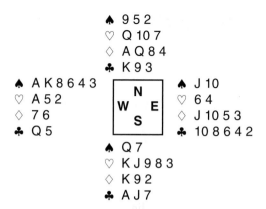

♠ 9 5 2
♡ Q 10 7
◊ A Q 8 4
♣ K 9 3

♠ A K 8 6 4 3
♡ A 5 2
◊ 7 6
♣ Q 5

N
W   E
S

♠ J 10
♡ 6 4
◊ J 10 5 3
♣ 10 8 6 4 2

♠ Q 7
♡ K J 9 8 3
◊ K 9 2
♣ A J 7

South plays in Four Hearts after West has made an overcall of One Spade. West leads the king of spades and continues with three rounds of the suit to kill dummy's nine. South plays hearts and West wins the second round and exits with a heart. Declarer has now the problem of avoiding a loser in clubs. There is a chance that the diamonds will break, and also the chance of a club finesse. Before testing the diamonds it is correct technique for South to play off the last trump, discarding a club from dummy. Three rounds of diamonds follow, but East is found to have the suit guarded. Then the king of clubs is led and another club; East plays the 10, but as he is known to have a diamond for his last card the finesse is refused and the doubleton queen is brought down – not by looking at West's hand but by counting East's.

Testing the lie

A hand like the last one is a perfect test of the difference between the player who goes ahead without thinking of what the other players hold, and the good player who explores every means to discover how the cards lie. The next hand is a slightly more advanced example of the same principle.

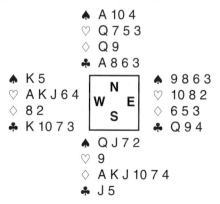

♠ A 10 4
♡ Q 7 5 3
◊ Q 9
♣ A 8 6 3

♠ K 5
♡ A K J 6 4
◊ 8 2
♣ K 10 7 3

N
W   E
S

♠ 9 8 6 3
♡ 10 8 2
◊ 6 5 3
♣ Q 9 4

♠ Q J 7 2
♡ 9
◊ A K J 10 7 4
♣ J 5

South plays in Five Diamonds after West has made an overcall of One Heart. As it happens, Three No-Trumps would have been an easier contract.

West leads the king of hearts, on which East plays the two. West then switches to diamonds and declarer takes two rounds, finishing in dummy. There is a reason for this. South can see that he may lose a trick in spades as well as in clubs. He wants to get a count on the spade suit, and an important preliminary is to find out how the clubs lie, if necessary by playing four rounds. When he leads clubs South wants the trick to be won by West, for it would interfere with his plans if he had to trump a lead of hearts from East.

So to the fourth trick a small club is led from dummy and the jack is won by West's king. West returns a club, won in dummy. Declarer ruffs a club, draws the last trump, and leads a low spade, finessing the ten. Then he leads the fourth club from dummy and discovers for certain that West started with four cards in this suit. West is known to have had two diamonds and in all probability, since he bid them, five hearts. So it is clear that West's king of spades is now single; accordingly South plays a small spade to the ace and not one of his honours. Had West turned up with only three clubs declarer would have placed him with three spades and 5-3-3-2 distribution; for remember that East played the two of hearts on the first trick, from which it was reasonable to infer that East had three hearts and not a doubleton.

Inference and hypothesis

The next hand shows something rather more difficult than anything we have met so far. Declarer's process of thought is carried one stage farther. The picture of an opponent's hand has to be based on a premise which is purely hypothetical.

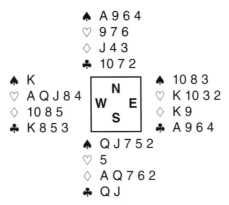

South made a third-hand opening of One Spade and West overcalled with Two Hearts. North raised to Two Spades and when East said Four Hearts

South bid Four Spades, which was passed all round. West opened with the three of clubs and East won with the ace. East returned the two of hearts; West won with the jack, cashed the king of clubs and led the ace of hearts. In actual play South led the queen of spades at this point, and although the diamonds lay favourably he went one down as he had to lose a trick in trumps. There was no reason to suppose that West had the king of spades alone, but nevertheless South should have played on that assumption. The reasoning is as follows:

The opposing clubs appear to be divided 4-4 and the hearts 5-4. Declarer cannot afford to lose a trick in diamonds, so he must assume that East has K-x and West x-x-x.

If this is in fact so, West can have only one spade.

If West has only one spade, then the only hope is that he has a singleton king.

Placing the cards

Inferences from the play sometimes make it possible to place the cards exactly, always a satisfying achievement. Declarer achieved a spectacular success on the following hand.

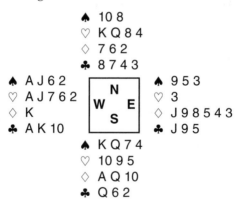

East/West were 40 up and West opened with a bid of Two Hearts. This was passed round to South, who to save the game hazarded Two Spades. West doubled and all passed. As West had opened with a Two-bid his double was for penalties rather than for a take-out.

The king of clubs was opened and when dummy went down South regretted his lack of caution; it looked as though he was in for a heavy penalty, for it was obvious from the bidding that East had a singleton heart. However, after the king of clubs had met with a discouraging discard, West led a low spade; the ten was played from dummy and a spade was led back. East should have petered in spades to show that he had a third trump and to suggest that he could ruff hearts. As East omitted to do this, West was still in difficulties. After long thought he led a small heart, not wishing to surrender control of the suit. South won in dummy with the king and dropped the ten from his own hand.

A diamond was led from dummy and before playing from his own hand South tried to count West's holding. No doubt West had five hearts, four spades, three clubs, and one diamond; the fact that he had not played a diamond to disembarrass himself of the lead strongly suggested that he held the lone king, so declarer went up with the ace and duly brought down the king. The queen of spades was laid down and the nine of hearts was led. West could still have defeated the hand by holding off this lead; however, he was somewhat rattled by this time, so he won with the ace, cashed his winning trump, and led another heart. South finessed the eight, discarded a club on the queen of hearts, and finessed the ten of diamonds to land a most unexpected contract.

Inferences from the play

It is easy to criticise West's defence in the hand just given, but he had in fact some difficult leads to make. The value of the hand lies in declarer's reasoning at the point when he led diamonds from dummy and placed the singleton king with West. To draw an inference of this kind is always the mark of a first-class player. Inferences abound in the play of every hand and the majority of players miss all but the most obvious. Every time a suit is played some sort of inference can be drawn; and equally the failure to play a suit tells a story of some kind.

When a suit is not played

What inference do you generally draw, as defender, when declarer at no-trumps refuses to touch a fairly strong suit in dummy, such as A-Q-J-x-x or A-Q-10-x-x-x?

It often happens that a defender who wins a trick halfway through the hand will attack this suit on the ground that since declarer has failed to play it he is unlikely to have the king. But that is very shallow reasoning. In practice a declarer who has not got the king of such a suit is sure to try to develop tricks early in the play. When declarer leaves the suit alone, it is fairly certain that he has the king and is seeking his ninth trick elsewhere.

The same sort of conclusion can be drawn when dummy has a fair holding headed by the K-Q, such as K-Q-10-x or K-Q-x-x-x. When declarer avoids playing such a suit, the most likely explanation is that he holds the ace.

A fairly precise inference can be drawn when such a holding in dummy as Q-J-x-x-x is neglected. Declarer is most unlikely to have the king; nor is it likely that he has A-x or A-x-x. He may have the singleton ace or a plain singleton. If he has more cards, he is likely to open up the suit.

Failure to touch K-J-x-x-x (or A-J-x-x-x) is significant. Declarer is most unlikely to have the queen. If he has x-x or x-x-x he will probably open up the suit. Quite a possible holding is A-x (or K-x); he may be exploring the other suits so as to find out how many tricks he needs from this suit.

When declarer fails to touch A-J-10-x or A-J-l0-x-x it is fairly certain that he holds the king; and he may hold the K-Q. Similar inferences can be drawn in regard to every combination of cards, and it is a very good exercise for a player to work them out for himself.

When a suit is played

When declarer does lead a suit, the defenders have a positive as well as a negative inference. If the contract is no-trumps, then it is reasonable to assume that declarer is fairly strong in whatever suit he attacks first. Defenders should not release their controls too soon. When a defender holds the ace of a suit over dummy's K-Q he is generally willing to hold up the ace on the first round; but when declarer leads from x-x-x in dummy and plays the king from his own hand, the left-hand defender seldom holds up the ace; yet, of course, it is most unlikely that declarer has the unsupported king. Many hands are much easier in play if the defenders can be persuaded to release their controls fairly early on. This is a typical example:

```
            ♠ 6 5
            ♡ K Q 10
            ◇ A 7 6 3
            ♣ A Q J 5
          ┌─────────┐
          │    N    │
          │ W     E │
          │    S    │
          └─────────┘
            ♠ K Q 3 2
            ♡ 8 7 3 2
            ◇ K Q 5
            ♣ 4 3
```

The jack of diamonds is led against Three No-Trumps and South wins in his own hand. Prospects seem good, for there are no obvious weaknesses; but after he has won the next three tricks with the king of hearts, king of spades, and queen of clubs, declarer is not too certain where he stands. No doubt the tricks can be made if he plays on the right suits; but by not being in a hurry to show where the cards lie the defenders make the play much more difficult for South.

The inferences which can be drawn from the play of a suit are of infinite variety. In all critical situations a player who has to choose between alternative lines of play should ask himself whether the view which he intends to take fits in with what he knows already. This endgame is a good example:

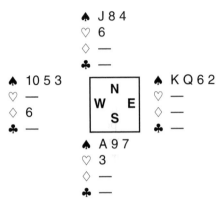

Hearts were trumps and South had created some sort of elimination position in which West had to lead. West led a low spade, dummy played low and East put on the king. South won with the ace, led a spade back and put up the jack, so losing two tricks in spades. Had he thought on the right lines, South would not have guessed wrongly on the second round. His play of the jack could win only if East held K-10-x of spades; and with such a holding East would, of course, have finessed the ten on the first round.

An interesting sidelight on this combination in spades is shown in this diagram:

```
            ♠ J 8 4
♠ Q 10 6 2            ♠ K 5 3
            ♠ A 9 7
```

If West has to open this suit, the lead of a low spade gives declarer no trouble. It is therefore a better shot for West to lead the queen. South wins with the ace and leads a low card on which West plays low. Now can South tell which card he should play from dummy? The answer is that had West held K-Q-x his natural play would have been a low card and not the king or queen. Therefore, unless he is up against a particularly resourceful defender, South should finesse the eight.

Tactical inferences

Certain inferences can be drawn from declarer's tactics on every hand. In a suit contract, declarer's handling of the trump suit is always significant. Suppose that declarer draws trumps without playing for ruffs in a suit of which dummy is short; there is a very strong inference here that declarer has no losers in the suit and probably is short himself. Defenders often fall victims to a pseudo-squeeze through failing to draw this particular inference.

When there is a long side suit in dummy and declarer makes no move to establish it, one of two inferences can be drawn: that his trump holding is not strong enough to enable him to ruff out the suit, or that his own holding in the suit is so weak that he sees no prospect of establishing it.

There is always an inference of some kind to be drawn when declarer does not draw trumps. He may want to ruff in dummy, or he may be preparing a complete cross-ruff.

At no-trumps the defenders should always study the direction of declarer's first line of attack. It was pointed out above that when declarer does not go for a good suit in dummy, it is probably because the suit is solid and he is looking elsewhere for the extra tricks which he needs. The same inference can be drawn when declarer refrains from playing a suit which he has bid strongly himself: probably the suit is solid and does not need to be developed.

Counting tricks in defence

The beginning and almost the end of good defensive play depends on keeping count of declarer's tricks and trying to work out his holding. Time and again a hand can be defeated if the defenders count and keep awake; often it is obvious that declarer is home if he holds a particular card: then the defenders' only hope is to assume that the declarer does not hold this card. Failure to count declarer's tricks leads players to discard very badly. That engaging writer, S.J. Simon, once drew a picture of this common failing which it would be impossible to surpass for economy of line.

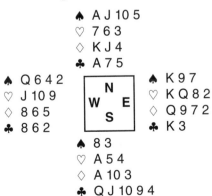

```
                    ♠ A J 10 5
                    ♡ 7 6 3
                    ◇ K J 4
                    ♣ A 7 5
  ♠ Q 6 4 2        ┌─────────┐      ♠ K 9 7
  ♡ J 10 9         │    N    │      ♡ K Q 8 2
  ◇ 8 6 5          │ W     E │      ◇ Q 9 7 2
  ♣ 8 6 2          │    S    │      ♣ K 3
                   └─────────┘
                    ♠ 8 3
                    ♡ A 5 4
                    ◇ A 10 3
                    ♣ Q J 10 9 4
```

The contract is Three No-Trumps and West leads the jack of hearts. Declarer holds up until the third round and then finesses a club. East wins, cashes the thirteenth heart and exits with a club. South has lost four tricks by this time, and if West is awake he can see that declarer has eight tricks on top – four clubs, two diamonds, one spade, and one heart. When the clubs are played out nine players out of ten in the West position will discard a couple of diamonds, arguing, no doubt, as Simon remarks, that the diamonds cannot take a trick and the queen of spades may. The point is that, knowing eight tricks are in the bag, West must credit his partner with the spade king. He should, therefore, discard his spades and hang on to the diamonds, so that South will have no clue which way to finesse for the queen.

Expert defenders often have recourse to what they call the 'advance trance'. They mean by this that they prefer to pause to consider their line of defence when a trick of no significance is played. So in the last example West should take his time about playing, not to the fourth or fifth round of clubs, but to the third round. Declarer's play is made much more difficult if the defenders do their thinking early on and give nothing away when their play becomes really difficult towards the end of a hand. A player who is in trouble over his discards can unguard an honour without much risk so long as he has steeled himself to do so three tricks before.

What's going on?

The whole lesson of this chapter has been that knowledge of the game and ability to execute brilliant coups count for very little compared with the consistent effort to follow what is going on among all four hands: how the cards are distributed and where the tricks are coming from. There is nothing very remarkable about the play of the following hand and yet a good player, having an off day, went wrong three times because he did not ask himself how declarer was going to find ten tricks.

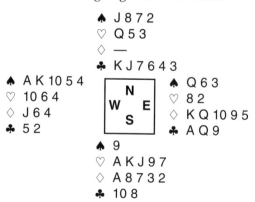

```
              ♠ J 8 7 2
              ♡ Q 5 3
              ◇ —
              ♣ K J 7 6 4 3
♠ A K 10 5 4        N        ♠ Q 6 3
♡ 10 6 4      W         E    ♡ 8 2
◇ J 6 4           S          ◇ K Q 10 9 5
♣ 5 2                        ♣ A Q 9
              ♠ 9
              ♡ A K J 9 7
              ◇ A 8 7 3 2
              ♣ 10 8
```

Having bid both hearts and diamonds, South became declarer in Four Hearts. West led the king of spades and East played the six. This was misguided, for East had no reason to encourage a spade continuation. However, West ignored the signal and made the correct play of a trump at the second trick. Declarer won and led the ten of clubs, West played the five, and East won with the queen.

At this point East had several possible lines of defence. A safe play to defeat the contract at once would have been ace and another club; West had shown a doubleton club by playing the five, so East knew that South would have to ruff the third round. South would be able to draw trumps and make dummy's long clubs, but that would give him only five tricks in trumps, three in clubs, and one in diamonds. Another possible defence was to lead the king of diamonds, so that when East won with ace of clubs he could play the queen of diamonds to force dummy and so prevent the clubs from being established. However, in practice East led a trump, which was perhaps the most obvious play, though not the best. Nevertheless, it was not fatal. Declarer won in his own hand and led a second club, which East won with the ace. The position was:

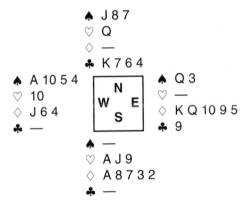

At this point a third club by East was essential. Instead, he played the queen of spades, thinking that the only hope was to find declarer with a second spade. To defend the hand to the best advantage East had to keep a careful count of declarer's possible tricks. The lead of the king of diamonds, when East was in for the first time, would have defeated the contract by two tricks, for South would have made only five top trumps, two ruffs, and the ace of diamonds.

2
The Strategy of Control

The struggle for control at no-trumps is generally between the long suits of the opposing sides; at suit contracts, between declarer's trumps and those of a defender. The principal weapon available to a declarer at no-trumps is hold-up play. The ordinary forms of hold-up play are too well known to need description, but there are many hands in which the decision whether or not to hold up depends upon considerations of strategy. This is almost always so when declarer has a combination of honours which includes the king and queen.

Hold-up with Q-x and K-x

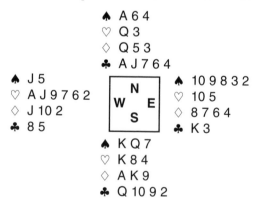

```
              ♠ A 6 4
              ♡ Q 3
              ◇ Q 5 3
              ♣ A J 7 6 4
  ♠ J 5              ♠ 10 9 8 3 2
  ♡ A J 9 7 6 2      ♡ 10 5
  ◇ J 10 2           ◇ 8 7 6 4
  ♣ 8 5              ♣ K 3
              ♠ K Q 7
              ♡ K 8 4
              ◇ A K 9
              ♣ Q 10 9 2
```

South reached a contract of Three No-Trumps and West, who had mentioned hearts during the bidding, led the seven. Declarer's play to the first trick is decided by the fact that the finesse in clubs must be taken towards East. The usual play with Q-x and K-x-x is to play the queen from dummy; but this is pointless here because the club finesse has to be taken towards East. So South plays low from dummy and allows East to win with the ten; East returns a heart but West never has a chance to run the suit.

It sometimes happens that declarer cannot tell which opponent has the first quick entry. He may have x-x in dummy of the suit led and K-J-x in his own hand; a small card is led and East plays the queen; it is right to duck only if it seems likely that West has no side entry.

When not to hold up

In Chapter 8 on Communication Plays examples are given of hands on which it is wrong to hold up because declarer has a chance to block the run of the opposing suit by winning the first lead. Sometimes it is wrong to hold up because the opponents are given a chance to switch to another and more dangerous suit. Declarer's play on the following hand needs careful thought.

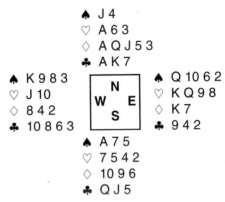

```
            ♠ J 4
            ♡ A 6 3
            ◇ A Q J 5 3
            ♣ A K 7
♠ K 9 8 3         N         ♠ Q 10 6 2
♡ J 10      W         E     ♡ K Q 9 8
◇ 8 4 2            S        ◇ K 7
♣ 10 8 6 3                  ♣ 9 4 2
            ♠ A 7 5
            ♡ 7 5 4 2
            ◇ 10 9 6
            ♣ Q J 5
```

South plays in Three No-trumps and the three of spades is led; the jack is played from dummy and East puts on the queen. Now the question is, should declarer hold up nor not? It seems at first that he should, for if East has three spades together with the king of diamonds, a hold-up of the ace of spades shuts out West. (It is, of course, from South's point of view, quite likely that West has led from a five-card suit.) This might be sound reasoning against weak opponents; but good players, after taking a couple of spade tricks, would certainly switch to hearts; South would then lose two spades and at least two hearts in addition to the king of diamonds.

Is there something to be said for holding up just for one round? If you work it out, this play cannot help. If West has five spades, then the hold-up for one round is useless: it simply gives East a chance to switch to hearts right away, setting up three tricks in the suit. If the spades are 4-4, then the hold-up is unnecessary, for the defence can take only three spades and the king of diamonds. So the answer is that South should win the opening lead of spades and trust that if the king of diamonds is wrong the spades will be evenly divided.

Hold-up with two controls

It is often correct, as any player knows who is not a beginner, to hold up
when declarer has two top cards in the suit led. However, this type of
hand calls for careful calculation, as the following example shows.

                    ♠ 8 6
                    ♡ Q 8 3
                    ◇ A K J 9 3
                    ♣ K 7 6

                    ♠ A K 4
                    ♡ K 9 7 2
                    ◇ 10 8 6
                    ♣ A 9 3

The opening lead against Three No-Trumps is the five of spades. Although
this is a very ordinary-looking hand, the right play is not at all easy to find.
If the diamonds are not all good, there are only eight tricks on top until the
ace of hearts has been cleared. Suppose first that South wins the first lead
and finesses diamonds, losing to East; the spades are then cleared and if
West has the ace of hearts the hand may be defeated. If South holds off the
first round, the contract is safe if East carries on with spades; but East, with
a spade trick in the bag, may switch to clubs and set up two tricks in this
suit together with a diamond, a heart and a spade.

There is only one way to make certain of the contract. The first lead of
spades should be won and a heart played. If the ace is not put on, South
switches at once to diamonds and makes game with at least four
diamonds, two spades, two clubs and one heart. If the ace of hearts is
played on the queen and spades are led, declarer holds up for one round;
the spade suit can then be cleared by the defence, but the diamonds can be
established without any risk of West obtaining the lead. If the spades are
4-4 the defenders take two spades, a heart and a diamond; if spades are 5-
3 West never gets in to play the long cards.

Hold-up at the cost of a trick

It is generally assumed that it is wrong to hold up with such a combination
as J-x in dummy and A-10-x in hand; for by winning the first trick declarer
stops the suit twice. A player must be on his guard against playing
automatically in a position like this:

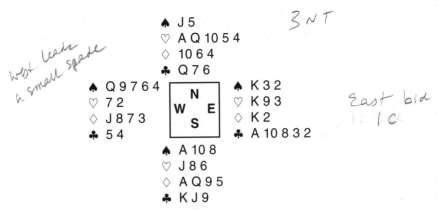

(handwritten annotations: "West leads a small spade", "3 NT", "East bid 1 C")

```
              ♠ J 5
              ♡ A Q 10 5 4
              ◇ 10 6 4
              ♣ Q 7 6
  ♠ Q 9 7 6 4      N       ♠ K 3 2
  ♡ 7 2          W   E     ♡ K 9 3
  ◇ J 8 7 3        S       ◇ K 2
  ♣ 5 4                    ♣ A 10 8 3 2
              ♠ A 10 8
              ♡ J 8 6
              ◇ A Q 9 5
              ♣ K J 9
```

South plays in Three No-Trumps after East has made an opening bid of One Club. In preference to leading his partner's suit West tries a small spade; the five is played from dummy and East puts on the king. The knowledge that both the king of hearts and ace of clubs must be held by East, who opened the bidding, should decide South to hold up even though this costs him a trick in spades. If South wins the first lead and attacks hearts, East will return a spade and West will duck; declarer cannot go game without clearing a trick in clubs, and when East comes in with the ace of clubs he will lead his third spade.

Control in suit contracts

The strategy of control in suit contracts is more complex than in no-trumps. At no-trumps, as we have seen, the problem centres around hold-up play. In suit contracts declarer has many ways of holding his own against a threatening array of trumps held by one of the defenders. Sometimes he has to avoid taking a finesse in trumps which he cannot afford to lose.

(handwritten: "4 S")

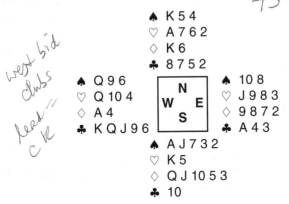

(handwritten annotations: "West bid clubs", "lead C K")

```
              ♠ K 5 4
              ♡ A 7 6 2
              ◇ K 6
              ♣ 8 7 5 2
  ♠ Q 9 6         N        ♠ 10 8
  ♡ Q 10 4      W   E      ♡ J 9 8 3
  ◇ A 4           S        ◇ 9 8 7 2
  ♣ K Q J 9 6              ♣ A 4 3
              ♠ A J 7 3 2
              ♡ K 5
              ◇ Q J 10 5 3
              ♣ 10
```

North/South reached a contract of Four Spades, West having bid clubs. The king of clubs is opened followed by another club, which declarer trumps. Now South must proceed with care; the situation is a very common one but it is easy to make a mistake. He should calculate that having lost a club he can afford to lose the ace of diamonds and a trump, but what he cannot afford is to take a losing finesse in trumps, be forced again in clubs, lose to the ace of diamonds and then again be forced in clubs; for West will still have a trump and South will have none left.

Game is a certainty, barring a 4-1 trump split, so long as South's timing is correct. He should play ace and king of trumps, leaving West with the good queen, and then clear the diamonds; West will win and play the queen of trumps, but South still has a trump left to deal with a club lead.

It is sometimes wise to make the opponents a possible present of a trump trick rather than risk conceding a valuable tempo. Declarer's play on the following hand illustrates this principle.

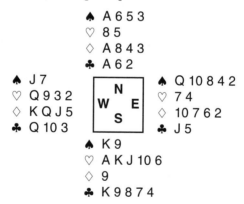

The contract was Four Hearts and West led the king of diamonds. Before taking trumps South rightly investigated his side suit; when both opponents followed to the ace and king of clubs, the time had come for a careful review of the position. Since only one club will be lost, declarer can afford to lose two tricks in trumps; he must realise, however, that he cannot afford to lose a trump finesse, be forced again and then find the trumps 4-2. As he can afford to lose two trump tricks he should play out the ace and king and then give up a club. West can force declarer with diamonds, but South carries on with clubs and West makes nothing more than two trump tricks.

Refusing to ruff

A fairly well-known stratagem to avoid losing control of trumps is to refuse to ruff until dummy can cope with the suit which the opponents have led:

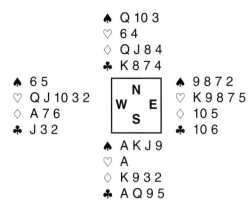

The queen of hearts is led against Four Spades. If declarer draws three or four rounds of trumps, the 4-2 split is fatal for him. The right play is to draw two rounds of trumps and then clear diamonds. West wins with the ace and plays a second heart; South discards a club from hand and any further heart leads can be dealt with in dummy.

In the play of that hand declarer used two stratagems to protect himself from losing control; one was to clear the side suit before drawing the trumps, and the other was to refuse to ruff the second heart.

Another way of keeping control of trumps is to give up tricks in the trump suit while dummy still has a trump left.

The following hand was played in a duplicate game at Four Hearts, doubled by East. The contract was defeated at every table, but analysis showed that it could have been made by correct play.

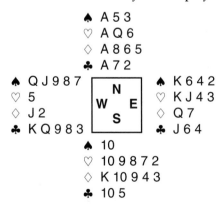

The queen of spades was led and won in dummy. If both hearts and diamonds break badly nothing can be done about the hand; South can, therefore, concentrate on overcoming a 4-1 trump distribution. The danger lies in the certainty of the spade force each time a trump trick is lost. Two forces will reduce South's trumps to three in length, one short of the number held by East. An inspiration followed by skilful play is needed to deal with the situation. The inspiration lies in realising that the run of the spades can be interrupted by dummy's trump ace, so long as that card is not played until East has won both his trump tricks. The play proceeds as follows: at the second trick the queen of hearts is played from dummy, East wins and leads a spade, declarer accepting the force; another heart is ducked and East wins with the jack. Another spade is played; South does not trump but discards his losing club; now if a fourth spade comes it is ruffed with the ace in dummy, South enters his hand by way of the king of diamonds, draws trumps and makes the rest.

Note that if declarer enters his hand with a diamond at trick two in order to take a heart finesse, he fails against best defence, as after ruffing with dummy's trump ace he cannot enter his own hand without forcing himself. His play cannot vary in any respect from that given; undoubtedly a difficult hand.

Handling a two-suiter

Two-suited hands raise special problems in trump control. The solution generally lies in dealing with the side suit before drawing trumps.

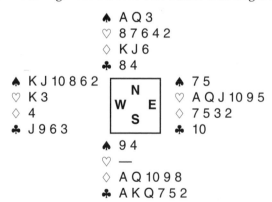

```
                  ♠ A Q 3
                  ♡ 8 7 6 4 2
                  ◇ K J 6
                  ♣ 8 4
  ♠ K J 10 8 6 2                  ♠ 7 5
  ♡ K 3             N             ♡ A Q J 10 9 5
  ◇ 4           W     E           ◇ 7 5 3 2
  ♣ J 9 6 3         S             ♣ 10
                  ♠ 9 4
                  ♡ —
                  ◇ A Q 10 9 8
                  ♣ A K Q 7 5 2
```

After some enterprising bidding South played in Six Diamonds, doubled by East for no very good reason. The king of hearts was opened and declarer was forced to ruff at once. In play he went down badly, and careful handling is needed to land the small slam.

It is apparent that, assuming the spade finesse is correct, the contract will be made if either minor suit breaks 3-2, provided the other is not worse than 4-1. In view of the bidding and the double it is probable that both suits will break badly, and South must concentrate on the problem of how to deal with the situation if both minor suits are 4-1. The difficulty is, of course, that if he has to lose a trick in clubs and the trumps are 4-1, he cannot sustain a force. In actual play declarer took two rounds of trumps, and when West failed he broached clubs, finessing a spade so as to lead the second round of clubs from dummy. East knew enough not to trump, and although South was able to ruff a losing club with dummy's third trump, he could not return to his own hand without ruffing, and disaster ensued.

The solution lies in tackling the clubs before the diamonds. One round of clubs is played, then dummy is entered with a trump and a second club is played from North; this is a regulation safety play to prevent a winning club being ruffed should East be short of them. If East ruffs this lead it will be his only trick; if he lets it pass, South wins, ruffs a club with one of dummy's high trumps and then returns to his own hand by means of a trump, making all thirteen tricks if he risks the spade finesse.

Establishing dummy's suit

In the process of establishing dummy's suit by ruffing, declarer sometimes loses control of the trump situation. On some hands this can be avoided by giving up an early trick in the suit which is being established.

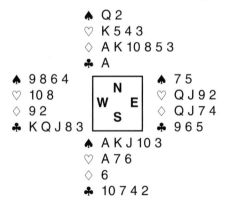

West leads the king of clubs against Six Spades and declarer must count his tricks carefully. It may seem at first count that twelve tricks can be made by way of five trumps, four top cards in the red suits, ace of clubs and two club ruffs. The difficulty in this line of play is that South is short of entries to his own hand. To make five tricks in trumps he has to risk ruffing the third round of diamonds with a low spade; if this card stands up, then the hand can be made more easily by establishing dummy's diamonds.

South should work out that he needs only four tricks from diamonds, so he need not take the risk of ruffing twice in his own hand. Best is to play ace and then a low diamond, allowing East to hold the trick. Whatever East plays, dummy is entered with the queen of spades. A diamond is ruffed and the trumps are drawn; then the king of hearts is an entry for the established diamond suit.

The play becomes very interesting if declarer plays ace, king and another diamond from dummy, ruffing with the three in his own hand. If West overruffs, the contract is made without difficulty; but if West makes the better play of discarding a heart, then declarer cannot get home. The refusal to overtrump conforms to a well recognised principle of defensive play.

3
Problems in Suit Play

In this chapter we examine various problems relating to the play at trump contracts. A constant stand-by for declarer is reverse dummy play.

Reverse dummy play

♠ 10 4 3
♡ A J 5
◇ K J 10
♣ Q J 8 3

♠ A J 9 5
♡ Q
◇ A Q 5 3
♣ A K 10 5

Only a beginner can be excused for going wrong in Six Clubs. The opening lead is a small heart, and as a finesse in hearts stands to gain nothing the ace should be played from dummy. Now it should be easy to see that there is a better play than to take two finesses in spades. South should ruff two hearts in his own hand, draw the trumps from dummy and lose only one spade.

Declarer should make it a regular practice to view a difficult hand from dummy's side as well as from his own. Many hands are quite simple to play if dummy is treated as the master hand. It often happens that declarer can obtain two ruffs in either hand, dummy or his own; when this is so it may depend upon entries which hand should be used for the ruffs.

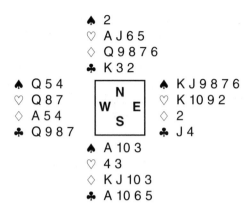

This was the bidding:

South	West	North	East
1♦	Pass	1♥	1♠
Pass	2♠	4♦	All Pass

As North/South had avoided a no-trump contract and North had shown an unbalanced hand, West opened with the ace of diamonds and followed with a second diamond. If South makes the mistake of going for spade ruffs in the long trump hand, he finds that there is also a fourth club to look after and that this cannot be ruffed without letting West into the lead to play a third round of trumps. Declarer's proper play is to duck a heart into East's hand and take two heart ruffs in his own hand, losing one heart, one diamond and one club.

Cross-ruff play

The principles of cross-ruff play are well known. In this form of play declarer has to count his tricks carefully and sometimes has to prepare for a cross-ruff by cashing winners in side suits.

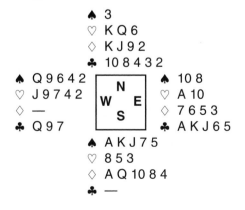

West opens with the queen of clubs against Five Diamonds and declarer ruffs. South has to choose between cross-ruffing and attempting to set up the spades. The cross-ruff is best, for if correctly handled it will succeed against a bad break in both spades and trumps. It is an important part of cross-ruffing technique that side winners should be cashed early before the defenders have a chance to discard. At the second trick, therefore, a heart is led; East wins with the ace and his best play is a trump; South holds the trick in his own hand, cashes two spades and a heart, and then makes seven more tricks by cross-ruffing. If South fails to set up his heart trick before ruffing spades, East can discard a heart and North cannot then make a trick in that suit.

A classic alternative

In the last example the play of a trump by the defenders at the third trick did not suffice to defeat the cross-ruff play. It often happens that a trump return in such a position leaves declarer with too few trumps to succeed by cross-ruffing, but gives him a chance to follow another line of play.

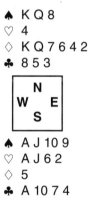

♠ K Q 8
♡ 4
◇ K Q 7 6 4 2
♣ 8 5 3

♠ A J 10 9
♡ A J 6 2
◇ 5
♣ A 10 7 4

This hand was given in a more elementary book than this, but the position which it illustrates is so common and so important that the hand can bear repeating.

A heart is led against Four Spades and declarer's first play should be a low diamond. It is invariably good play to tackle early on a side suit which has to be played sooner or later. If the king of diamonds wins in dummy declarer is home on a cross-ruff; he should cash the ace of clubs and claim seven more tricks by way of cross-ruffing.

If East wins the diamond lead and returns a club, South should win, enter dummy by ruffing a heart, and play the queen of diamonds; if this stands up, he is home as before on the cross-ruff, making seven trumps and one trick in each of the side suits.

Finally, suppose that East wins the diamond and finds the correct defence of a trump return. Counting his tricks, South should realise that he has now not enough for a cross-ruff game to succeed; the trump lead restricts him to six tricks in spades. The only hope now is to find a 3-3 break in both diamonds and spades; the trump return is won in dummy, and queen and a small diamond are played. If diamonds break, declarer stakes all on drawing the trumps in three rounds. If the diamonds split 4-2 then South plays a cross-ruff and accepts one down. The play is not difficult on this hand; all that declarer has to do is to count his tricks carefully and plan the play accordingly.

Playing on dummy's suit

The next hand also shows the defenders faced with two alternatives; either they force the dummy and allow a cross-ruff, or they play trumps and allow declarer to win tricks with dummy's suit.

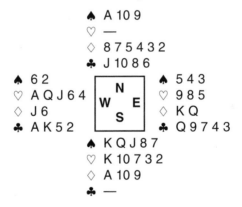

The king of clubs is led against Four Spades and declarer ruffs. An unthinking player would start forthwith on a cross-ruff game, not taking the trouble to observe that this line of play inevitably leaves him one trick short. As usual, it is right to play the long side suit first, so ace and another diamond are played. East wins and his return is clearly marked: with the threat of the established diamonds confronting him, he should lead a heart to force the dummy. The ten fetches the jack, and now it is up to South to refuse this apparent gift of a ruff in dummy; he should discard a club, leaving West in a hopeless position. If West plays a club, an overtrick can be made by ruffing clubs twice and discarding the nine of diamonds on the third trump in dummy. If West plays a heart he sets up declarer's tenth trick, the rest of the hand being played on a cross-ruff; and if West plays a trump, declarer leads a second round of trumps and then the third diamond; East can trump this but it is his last trick. Both sides have an opportunity for good play.

Loser-on-loser play

Two examples follow of the loser-on-loser theme which will be found to
recur throughout the chapters on endplays. The first example shows a
situation which is a blind spot for a large number of players.

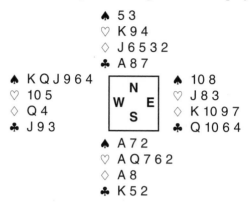

North/South reach Four Hearts after West has made an overcall of One
Spade. The king of spades is led and declarer wins the second round,
noting East's peter. There are nine tricks on top if the trumps break, and the
tenth must come from a ruff or from a long diamond. But the spade is likely
to be overruffed and the diamonds may well not break evenly. The best
plan is to lead a third spade and throw on it one of dummy's clubs; then
the extra trick can be safely picked up by ruffing a club. Despite its essential
simplicity this play is very often missed; most players would take two
rounds of hearts and hope that East could not overtrump the third spade.

Most players know the danger of overruffing a defender at the cost of a
trump trick. When possible, declarer should throw a loser rather than
overruff when his trump suit is not solid. Here is a difficult example of this
type of play:

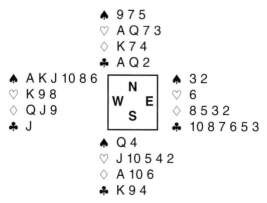

South plays in Four Hearts and the defenders start off with three rounds of spades. Although West's third spade is a master, it is, of course, good play by East to put on his six of trumps on the offchance that it may force a valuable trump from declarer. Improbable though it seems that the six can do any good, the fact is that if South overruffs he cannot make the contract, for he has to lose a trump to West as well as a diamond. The right play for declarer is not to trump but to throw a losing diamond. Then he can finesse against the king of hearts and make all the remaining tricks.

A 4-3 trump fit

There is one class of hand of which bridge writers seem to fight shy, although they are perhaps a greater test of a player's skill than any other type. These are the hands in which declarer has a shaky trump suit, divided 4-3.

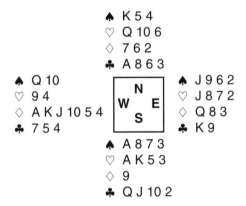

The bidding goes as follows:

South	West	North	East
1♣	1♢	2♣	Pass
Pass	2♢	Pass	Pass
2♡	Pass	Pass	3♢
Pass	Pass	3♡	All Pass

The bidding is fairly typical of matchpoint tactics; had North been sure that his partner had four clubs he might have preferred to make clubs the final bid.

Diamonds are led and continued, and South has no option but to ruff. Obviously it would be a mistake to play trumps, so the next move should be a club finesse; East wins and plays a spade; this is as good a defence as any, for declarer is quite willing to trump another diamond. In fact, South should manoeuvre for this himself; he should win the spade in his own hand, draw ace and king of trumps, enter dummy with the ace of clubs, and ruff a diamond. At this point the position is:

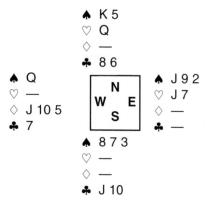

South can afford to lose two more tricks and should not make the mistake of entering dummy and trying to draw the trumps. East has turned up with three diamonds to the queen and probably four spades to the jack; as he gave a lift to Three Diamonds, it is likely that his distribution is 4-4-3-2 rather than 4-3-3-3. Also, on the second round of clubs East dropped the nine. So the right play is to lead clubs; East ruffs, but dummy regains the lead to draw the last trump and win the fourth round of clubs. So by careful play South makes Three Hearts, losing only one trick in each suit. It is the sort of hand on which first-class players seldom fail and average players never succeed.

Overcoming a bad break

Some players are put right out of their stride by a bad break in trumps. This chapter ends with a hand which is certainly difficult but is instructive because it combines many forms of play and leads to an interesting end game.

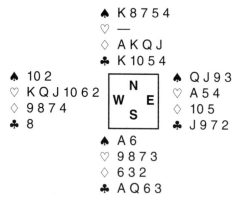

West, not vulnerable, made a pre-emptive opening of Three Hearts; as often happens, this caused the opponents to bid with all the more determination and they reached Six Clubs, which East doubled on the strength of his holding in the black suits. West led the king of hearts and dummy ruffed.

It is far from being an easy hand to play, especially as the trumps are likely to be 4-1. Declarer's first idea should be to play on the dummy, ruffing two spades in his own hand. One round of trumps should be played, to prevent a possible overruff by West; if the trumps are 5~0, then the hand is unlikely to be made anyway. So the ace of clubs is played and three rounds of spades follow; then a diamond, followed by another spade ruff, and another diamond. The position is:

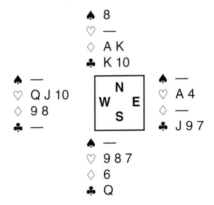

```
              ♠ 8
              ♡ —
              ◇ A K
              ♣ K 10
♠ —                          ♠ —
♡ Q J 10      ┌─────────┐     ♡ A 4
◇ 9 8         │    N    │     ◇ —
♣ —          │ W     E │     ♣ J 9 7
              │    S    │
              └─────────┘
              ♠ —
              ♡ 9 8 7
              ◇ 6
              ♣ Q
```

In this position the fifth spade is led from dummy. If East ruffs, South overruffs and leads a diamond, the dummy hand being high except for one trump loser. So East does best to discard on the eight of spades; South throws a diamond and then leads a diamond from dummy; if East discards on this trick South can either discard himself or ruff with the queen and bring the play to a spectacular conclusion with a trump endplay against East.

PART TWO
MAINLY DEFENCE

4

Choosing a Lead

Among the traditions of teaching in bridge, none is less worthy than that which prescribes for opening leads an order of preference based upon the character of a player's holding in the various suits. Always in the place of honour at the head of the list is the combination A-K-Q. It is followed by such dependable characters as K-Q-J, Q-J-10, and singleton-of-partner's-suit at a trump contract. Then the rank and file – top of nothing, fourth best, the untrusted doubleton; finally, the despised tail - A-Q-x, K-J-x, singleton king, and the like.

It is all quite ridiculous because every player of any experience and judgement knows that there are hundreds of times when these conventional preferences are no guide at all to the choice of the best lead.

This is not an attack on the conventions in leading themselves. These were established in the days of whist and were based on sound enough principles. In the days when there was no bidding and trumps were determined arbitrarily, a player had no chance to form a view concerning the course which play might take and his choice of lead was naturally determined by what he held in different suits.

At contract bridge the player on lead has a good deal of information. Even if the bidding has been no more informative than 1NT - 3NT, he has more to go on than at auction bridge when he would have had nothing but a bid of One No-Trump from the first player. If the bidding is 1NT – 2NT – 3NT, he knows this much extra, that the declarer is unlikely to have much in hand; so the best hope of defeating the contract may well lie in following a passive course and not giving tricks away.

No suggestion for improving the game could be more inept than that which recommends that the dummy be exposed before the so-called 'blind lead' is made. Blind leads are for deaf players. There is great scope for judgement in the choice of opening lead; to judge well, the player must attend to the bidding very carefully and in the light of this bidding and of his own holding must try to foresee what type of hand it is going to be.

Does it look as though the contract is safe unless a desperate chance comes off? Must defenders hurry to find tricks in side suits? Is there any positive advantage in trump leads? At no-trumps, is the leader to play to set up a suit of his own, or the suit of his partner, or is it best to sit on the fence and leave declarer to find his own tricks?

Leading against no-trumps

At certain times in bridge history the traditional lead of fourth best against no-trumps lost favour. Unless they had a five-card suit players tended to prefer a top-of-nothing lead in a side suit to the lead of fourth best from a four-card suit headed by a tenace combination. There was much talk of 'the modern theory of leads'. Now in turn there has been a reaction against short-suit leads. Probably the right way to regard this problem is to say that the lead of the longest and strongest suit should be preferred unless there is a good reason to reject it. A tenace holding does not of itself constitute a good reason.

The player on lead should try to judge what prospect he has of establishing his long suit and whether a safe lead or an attacking lead is indicated. Study this bidding:

West	East
1♣	1♠
2♣	2NT
3NT	Pass

As South you have to lead from:

> ♠ A Q 5
> ♥ J 8 6 2
> ♦ 7 4
> ♣ Q 7 6 3

It is clear from the bidding that you must attack, because there is a long suit on your left which declarer will no doubt try to establish. Most players would recognise this and would lead the fourth best heart, even though a lead away from a jack is more likely to cost a trick than a lead from any other honour. Nevertheless, in this example the lead of the two of hearts would be correct.

Now suppose instead that you had to lead against the same bidding from:

> ♠ Q 5 3
> ♥ J 8 6 2
> ♦ 7 4
> ♣ Q 7 6 3

The hand is the same except that the ace of spades has been taken away. You still have to find an attacking lead, but the best attack no longer lies in hearts. Your own hand is too weak to make it likely that you will get this suit going; the best chance lies in a diamond lead, made not for safety, but because it looks as though the best hope is to find your partner strong in diamonds.

The time to make a neutral lead which is unlikely to give a trick away is when it looks as though the opponents' contract is in the balance and it does not seem probable that there are long suits about. The bidding has gone:

West	East
—	1♥
2♥	2NT
3NT	Pass

You are South again and you have to lead from:

♠ K Q 7 5
♥ 8 4 2
♦ Q 9 7 4
♣ 6 3

You can judge from the bidding that the opponents cannot have much to spare. It is also unlikely that either opponent has a five-card suit. There is no need to hurry for tricks; a lead from either of your long suits may well cost a trick and you should look for a safe lead. Most players having reached this point in their reasoning, would lead a club; but this, too, is a lead which can well cost a trick, for partner very likely has four clubs and your lead may damage his hand. The safe lead is a heart – the enemy suit. You leave declarer to find his tricks, and there must be a fine chance that after making his heart winners declarer will find the rest of the hand uphill work. Had the bidding been: 1NT – 3♥ – 3NT there would have been no reason to play safe. The best chance would be to lead a spade.

When to depart from fourth highest

Some players make it a practice always to lead the lowest card their long suit. It is, of course, easy to find examples in which the fourth best lead helps declarer more than partner. For all that, the convention is a sound one in general, for it is more important to give information to partner than to conceal it from an opponent. There are some occasions, however, when it is good strategy to depart from the ordinary convention.

The bidding by the opponents has been: 1♥ – 2NT – 3NT and you have to make the opening from:

♠ K 8 6 5 2
♥ A 8
♦ Q 6 2
♣ K 8 4

There is a lot to be said for the lead of the two of spades rather the five. It is clear from the strength of your hand that partner has little, so it is unlikely to matter if you mislead him. Your object should be to conceal from declarer the danger which your suit and general strength represent. If you lead a card which seems to show that you have only a four-card suit, declarer may take a view in the play and finesse towards you in the minor suits. An alternative plan is to lead the five, but on the next round to play the six and not the two.

Occasionally it may be good strategy to avoid the lead of fourth best when you have only four cards. The bidding is the same as in the last example (1♥ – 2NT – 3NT) and you have to lead from:

♠ K 6 5 2
♥ 9 8 5
♦ A 6 2
♣ 8 6 4

You have no good reason for leading anything but a spade. It may turn out to be a clever move to lead the five rather than the two. This hand, as opposed to the last, has no cards in the minor suits which can be described as possible entries; of course the ace of diamonds is a certain entry, but the point is that you have no cards which might win a finesse. By leading the five of spades and following with the two you give declarer the impression that you have a five-card suit, and this may cause him to take finesses in the minor suits into the wrong hand.

Leading dummy's suit

In the last example a lead which some players would have considered is a heart through the suit bid by dummy. This is very seldom good tactics. Even if partner is fairly strong in the suit, the only effect of such a lead by the defence is to give up a valuable tempo. Some players regularly make this lead through a suit bid by dummy when nothing else appeals to them. It is generally a very bad lead.

Only with a holding such as the following is a lead through dummy's suit to be recommended:

♠ K J 9
♥ 9 4
♦ A J 8 3
♣ K J 6 2

There seems little chance that partner can give you much help in the defence to Three No-Trumps. So it may be best to lead a heart through dummy and leave declarer to find his own tricks.

Leading against suit contracts

As a rule the first point which a defender has to decide is whether he should make a safe or an attacking lead. Often against the same contract the lead from the same hand may be different according to the way in which the contract is reached. Suppose the bidding has been 1♠ – 3♠ – 4♠, and you have to lead from:

> ♠ 8 7
> ♥ K 5 2
> ♦ Q 9 6 4 3
> ♣ Q 5 2

You don't know much about the hand, but as no side suits have been bid you should choose a safe lead. Probably a trump is less likely to give a trick away than any other lead, and there is a chance that may have some positive value.

Now suppose instead that in the course of reaching Four Spades the opponent on your left has twice bid clubs. It is imperative to look for tricks before declarer can get the clubs going. The best lead is a heart. It may turn out, of course, that declarer has something like A-Q of hearts; but if this is so it still remains unlikely that you have given a vital trick.

The lead of the small heart in the last example could not be described as a desperation lead. Most players are willing to take a chance every now and again from a holding such as K-x. For against a confidently bid Three Clubs, the most likely looking lead from:

> ♠ K 5
> ♥ Q 9 7 5 2
> ♦ K 8 3
> ♣ 6 4 2

is the king of spades. But it would be a mistake to lead this card against Five Clubs, for if partner has the ace of spades you have a good chance of defeating the contract anyway, so there is no need to risk so dangerous a lead.

A constructive lead

There is one lead which looks dangerous but is not so in fact. You hold:

♠ A Q 10 7
♥ 9 8
♦ Q 6 4
♣ J 5 3 2

and you have to lead against Four Hearts after an opening bid of One No-Trump has been made by the player on your left. Your lead should be the queen of spades. The king is marked with the player on your left, so there is no danger of the lead giving a trick away; it may prove a fine attacking lead if declarer has J-x-x, for as soon as your partner gets in he can lead a small spade and set up two tricks in the suit.

Leads to force declarer

All experienced players know that a forcing game is stronger than any other defence. The lead against Four Spades from a hand such as:

♠ 9 6 5 3
♥ K 10 8 6 4
♦ 5
♣ K 8 3

depends upon whether or not the bidding suggests that a forcing game may succeed. If dummy has shown four trumps, then a forcing game is useless and the singleton diamond is the best lead. But if dummy has given only delayed support, then declarer may have five spades and dummy only two or three. If this is so, the best chance for the defence lies in forcing declarer and the best lead is a low heart.

Although most players can see the possible advantage of forcing tactics when they have four trumps themselves, they tend to overlook the same possibility when partner can be placed with trumps.

Study this bidding:

West	East
—	1♠
2♣	2♥
2♠	4♠
Pass	

You have to lead from:

> ♠ 5
> ♥ 10 8 3
> ♦ A Q 10 4 2
> ♣ Q 7 5 2

There must be a good chance that partner holds four trumps. The only suit in which you may be able to force declarer to ruff is diamonds, and the ace of diamonds is your best lead.

When to lead trumps

One can often judge from the bidding that declarer is going to play a cross-ruff game. The bidding goes:

West	East
—	1♣
1♠	2♦
2NT	3♣
3♦	Pass

As South, you hold:

> ♠ K J 10 6
> ♥ 8 6 4 2
> ♦ Q 8 5
> ♣ A J

In the bidding West has put his partner back to diamonds although this is obviously East's shorter suit. No doubt West has a singleton club. The danger of a cross-ruff is obvious, and South should lead a diamond. It is true that the lead may cost a trick in trumps. But as you will be able to lead diamonds twice before any ruffing starts, you will get your trick back; and if your partner holds one of the top honours in diamonds you may be able to draw three rounds of trumps and defeat the contract by several tricks.

When declarer has shown a second suit and one of the suits has been supported, the defenders are generally on the look-out for a trump lead, but often a trump is led when it is not necessary. The bidding goes:

West	East
—	1♠
2♣	2♥
2♠	4♠
Pass	

South has to lead from:

♠ 8 2
♥ Q 10 6 4
♦ K J 3
♣ J 8 5 2

Most players would lead a trump, being influenced by their strong holding in declarer's second suit. But probably your partner is short in hearts as well as dummy; he will, therefore, be able to overruff dummy, so that there is no great need for trump leads by the defence. The right shot here is a small diamond; it may be necessary to set up tricks in this suit before declarer can obtain discards on dummy's clubs.

The time for a trump lead against declarer's two-suiter is when the leader is short in declarer's side suit. Suppose that bidding is as before:

West	East
—	1♠
2♣	2♥
2♠	4♠
Pass	

This time South holds:

♠ 6 4 2
♥ Q 3
♦ K J 5 4
♣ J 8 5 2

Now the prospect of a successful cross-ruff game by declarer is more threatening. It is plain that East will be able to ruff hearts in dummy with impunity, for North will have to follow suit on the third and possibly fourth round of hearts. So now a trump lead is called for; the best hope for the defenders is that they will regain the lead before the cross-ruff starts and will be able to play a second round of trumps.

Forcing a no-trump game

It sometimes happens in the bidding that one side is doubled early on and is driven from pillar to post until it settles in some uneasy contract at a low level. Try to follow this rather complicated sequence:

South	West	North	East
—	1NT	Pass	Pass
Dble	Pass	Pass	2♣
Pass	Pass	Dble	2♠
Dble	All Pass		

As South, you hold:

♠ K Q 6 3
♥ A 8 4
♦ A 10 7 2
♣ Q 8

You see what has happened: you have doubled the opening bid of One No-Trump on your left and the player on your right has bid clubs, doubled by your partner, and then spades, doubled by yourself. Obviously you have them on the run. The way to obtain a maximum set is to force a no-trump game on the opponents from the first. The only way in which East/West are likely to scramble five or six tricks is by making some of their small trumps; so your best lead, as South, is the three of spades.

A trump lead from a long suit

When a player has a long string of trumps, it is generally good tactics to lead a trump. For example, sometimes the player on lead holds five trumps and can judge from the bidding that the opponents have four trumps each; then a trump lead is almost always the best tactics. To realise that this must be so, put yourself in the position of declarer with four trumps in his own hand and four trumps in dummy who finds that the opposing trumps are divided 5-0; the one thing he will not do is to continue trump leads. A low trump is often a good lead from K-x-x-x and also from Q-x-x-x.

When the opening leader is lucky enough to hold better trumps than declarer, it is generally good policy to draw trumps. Suppose that after partner has opened One Spade you have to lead against Two Hearts doubled, holding:

♠ Q J 4
♥ K J 10 9 8 6
♦ J 10 7
♣ 3

Clearly you do not want declarer to have the chance to make his low trumps by ruffing. Your best lead is actually the king of hearts. There might be a singleton queen on the table.

Trump lead after a penalty pass

Sometimes it is possible to place partner with a strong holding in trumps; this happens when partner has made a pass of a take-out double. The player on your right opens One Heart, you double, and all pass. You hold:

♠ K Q 10 4
♥ 6 5
♦ Q J 9 4
♣ A K 3

To make a penalty pass when sitting under the bidder, your partner should hold a long and strong sequence in trumps. The best defence is to pick up declarer's small trumps, and your opening lead should be the six of hearts.

Leads against a slam contract

It is a fairly well-known principle that a player should look for a safe lead against a grand slam, and an attacking lead against a small slam. Suppose that you have to lead against Six Spades after the bidding:

West	East
1♦	1♠
3♣	3♠
4NT	5♠
6♠	

As South, you hold:

♠ 7 3
♥ K J 7 4
♦ J 8
♣ Q 6 5 4 2

Declarer has bid nothing but spades, dummy has bid diamonds and clubs. Your best lead is the four of hearts; you hope that your side will be able take a trick in diamonds or spades and you have to try to set up early trick in hearts.

Had the final contract of Six Spades been doubled by your partner, you would have had to look for a surprise lead. Most players use the Lightner Slam Double convention, whose effect is that a player who doubles a slam contract is asking partner to find a lead other than the normal one. In this example the normal lead is a heart, the unbid suit. So the double asks for something different. Probably partner wants a club; it does not follow from West's bid of Three Clubs that he has a genuine suit; it may be that partner has A-K of clubs and that it is necessary to win a club before any discards can be taken. Quite often a Lightner double is made to show that the leader's partner has a void somewhere; had West made an opening bid of One Club in this example, the explanation of a double of Six Spades might well be that North was void in clubs and was trying to show this by the double.

5

Promoting Tricks in Defence

This chapter describes, without reference to general tactics, a number of situations in which the defenders can promote an extra trick in a single suit, often the trump suit. In the establishment of side-suit tricks there are certain forms of play used by defenders which are seldom made by declarer. Consider, for example, the defender's problem in the following position:

The hands of West and North are:

```
                    ♠ K 10 4
                    ♡ 10 6 3 2
                    ◇ A Q 10 5
                    ♣ Q 6
    ♠ J 9 8 5      ┌─────────┐
    ♡ K 8 4        │    N    │
    ◇ K 7 4        │ W     E │
    ♣ A 9 3        │    S    │
                   └─────────┘
```

The bidding has gone:

South	North
1♣	1◇
1NT	3NT
Pass	

West leads the five of spades and dummy's king wins, East playing the two. Declarer plays queen and another club, the king losing to the ace. East has played the two of clubs and then the seven. The problem is, what should West lead and why?

The play so far has shown that South holds A-Q of spades and five clubs to the K-J. (This much can be deduced as follows: had East the queen of spades he would not have played the two; had East held Q-2 alone, South would have let the first trick come up to his A-7-6-3. The fact that East did not signal to show four clubs, together with South's play of the suit, makes it certain that South started with five to the K-J; had they been headed by K-10 he would have finessed the ten.)

It is, therefore, certain that South can go game with four clubs, three spades and two diamonds, unless the defence can take four tricks in hearts. This can be done even if South holds as much as Q-9 of provided that West leads the eight; if West leads the four East, holding A-J-7-5 will win with the ace and return the five, but the suit will then blocked. So the correct play for West is the eight of hearts and no other card.

This position is not so easy to recognise from the other side.

10 6 5 2

A 9 4   K J 7 3

Q 8

If East is on lead and judges that his partner holds the ace, the only card he can play to win four tricks straight off is the king; West has to unblock with the nine.

There are a number of situations in which the defenders use the tactics of a backward finesse. This is the most simple:

10 8 4

A 3 2   K J 9 7

Q 6 5

When he attacks this suit, East must lead the jack to win four tricks. Essentially the same play is made in this position:

A J 2

Q 10 7 4   K 8 5

9 6 3

The way for West to attack the suit is to lead the ten; any other lead gives declarer a double stop.

From a combination headed by A-Q the queen is generally the right lead:

K 7 5

A Q 10 4   9 8 3

J 6 2

So long as partner has an entry, West establishes three tricks by leading the queen. The same play has to be made if this diagram is viewed the other way up:

J 7 3

10 8 5   A Q 9 4

K 6 2

East attacks the suit by leading the queen.

The lead through A-Q from a combination headed by K-J is generally the jack:

A Q 2

K J 7 3   9 8 4

10 6 5

If West plays the suit he must lead the jack and not a small card. The defenders often miss their way in a situation like this:

8 5 2

K J 9 4   Q 3

A 10 7 6

East is on lead and has no other entry. He places partner with strength in this suit and also with outside entries. The usual play by East is the queen, but it can be a mistake; declarer wins and if East has no other entry the suit is stopped twice. If East leads small on the other hand, West can win with the nine and play a small card back; in this way the defenders come to three tricks in the suit. Situations of this kind are sometimes difficult to judge in play; if the cards lie rather differently, the queen may be best.

Preserving a tenace position

The defensive play required in the following hand proved a blind spot for most players when the hand was set in a contest with prepared hands.

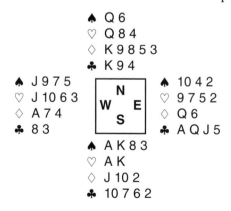

West leads the three of hearts against Three No-Trumps. South wins and finesses the jack of diamonds, losing to East's queen. As South has bid spades, East can see little future in this suit and it is obvious that the setting tricks can come only from clubs. Most players thought they were achieving their par when they played back the queen of clubs. However, this is not good enough, for as the cards lie South has a second stop after this play. The only return to establish three certain tricks in clubs is the low one; then, when West wins with ace of diamonds, he leads a second club and East makes three tricks to set the contract.

Second hand low or high

One of the most difficult decisions which a defender has constantly to make is when declarer leads low to a suit in dummy headed by K-Q or K-J, and the player underneath the dummy has the ace. The defender has to gauge whether declarer has led a singleton or not; and also whether, if the lead is a singleton, it is better to go in with the ace or hold it up. Sometimes it is almost impossible for a defender to judge, especially if the play is made early on before the defenders have a count of the hand. For this reason a declarer with K-J-x-x-x in dummy and a doubleton or singleton in his own hand should play the suit at the first opportunity – before the defenders can be sure whether it is better to play the ace or not.

A defender cannot do the right thing every time in these positions, but it is probably correct to say that when in doubt it is better to play low; for even when the lead is a singleton, it is often a mistake to play the ace. This hand is a rather striking example:

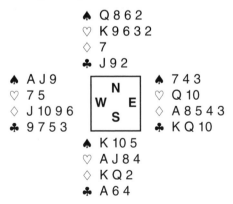

The bidding has gone:

South	North
1♡	2♡
2NT	4♡
Pass	

The jack of diamonds is led, and if you look at the hand you will see that East can beat the contract only by not playing his ace at the first trick. East can see that if he puts on the ace of diamonds, declarer's K-Q will provide discards for two losing clubs; by giving up one diamond the defenders gain two tricks in clubs.

Playing partner for a ruff

Now we come to the first of a series of examples in which play slightly outside the usual is needed to win extra tricks in the trump suit. Most players can see ahead when they want to ruff themselves, but they tend to miss chances of giving partner a ruff.

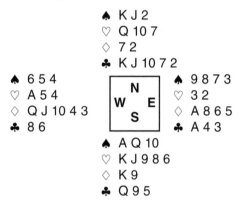

```
                    ♠ K J 2
                    ♡ Q 10 7
                    ◇ 7 2
                    ♣ K J 10 7 2
    ♠ 6 5 4            N            ♠ 9 8 7 3
    ♡ A 5 4        W     E          ♡ 3 2
    ◇ Q J 10 4 3       S            ◇ A 8 6 5
    ♣ 8 6                           ♣ A 4 3
                    ♠ A Q 10
                    ♡ K J 9 8 6
                    ◇ K 9
                    ♣ Q 9 5
```

The bidding has gone:

South	North
1♡	2♣
3♣	3♡
4♡	Pass

West leads the queen of diamonds and East wins with the ace. What should he play back? The contract can be defeated only if West has a trump trick. West can hardly have a trick in spades as well as a trick in trumps, but there is a good chance that a second trick may be won by means of a club ruff. Remember that South has raised clubs; West is not likely to have a singleton club, for with a singleton and a high trump he would have led the singleton. If West has a doubleton club, as it is reasonable to suppose, the hand is defeated by the return of a low club at the second trick.

Refusing to overruff

In the handling of the trump suit itself there are numerous ways in which defenders can come to extra tricks. One of the best known is the refusal to overtrump in a position such as the following:

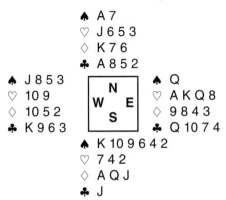

```
              ♠ A 7
              ♡ J 6 5 3
              ◇ K 7 6
              ♣ A 8 5 2
♠ J 8 5 3                    ♠ Q
♡ 10 9          N            ♡ A K Q 8
◇ 10 5 2     W     E         ◇ 9 8 4 3
♣ K 9 6 3       S            ♣ Q 10 7 4
              ♠ K 10 9 6 4 2
              ♡ 7 4 2
              ◇ A Q J
              ♣ J
```

Against a contract of Three Spades the defenders start off with four rounds of hearts. Declarer ruffs the fourth round with the ten; it would be bad play for West to overruff, even though he does not know about his partner's queen. So long as West discards on this trick he comes to two tricks in trumps.

Many players miss the right line when they have a chance, which they should refuse, to overruff the dummy.

```
              10
8 4                         K J 7 2
           A Q 9 6 5 3
```

This is the trump suit and declarer ruffs a side suit with dummy's ten of trumps. If East overruffs, he makes only two tricks in the trump suit but if he discards instead of overruffing, he can make three tricks in trumps. There are innumerable variations of this play.

Promoting tricks by ruffing

A very well-known manoeuvre in defence is to give partner a chance to ruff and so force the declarer to use a high trump. This play is known as the 'uppercut'. Two examples follow which are rather out of the ordinary.

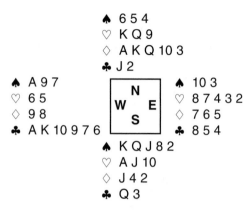

♠ 6 5 4
♡ K Q 9
◇ A K Q 10 3
♣ J 2

♠ A 9 7
♡ 6 5
◇ 9 8
♣ A K 10 9 7 6

♠ 10 3
♡ 8 7 4 3 2
◇ 7 6 5
♣ 8 5 4

♠ K Q J 8 2
♡ A J 10
◇ J 4 2
♣ Q 3

Against Four Spades West wins the first two tricks with the king and ace of clubs. Dummy's holding in the red suits is so strong that it is clear that no more tricks can be won outside trumps. The only hope lies in promoting a second trump. So although West knows that his partner has the other club, he leads a third round so that later East will be able to ruff the fourth round. When trumps are played, West wins with the ace and plays a fourth club which East ruffs with the ten of spades; then West's nine of spades becomes the setting trick.

Double trump promotion

Declarer's trump holding seems to be invulnerable in the next example, but nevertheless he had to lose two tricks in the suit.

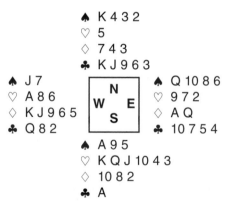

♠ K 4 3 2
♡ 5
◇ 7 4 3
♣ K J 9 6 3

♠ J 7
♡ A 8 6
◇ K J 9 6 5
♣ Q 8 2

♠ Q 10 8 6
♡ 9 7 2
◇ A Q
♣ 10 7 5 4

♠ A 9 5
♡ K Q J 10 4 3
◇ 10 8 2
♣ A

Defending Three Hearts, West leads a low diamond to East's ace and overtakes his partner's return of the queen. As South has shown a strong hand in the bidding, West judges that the setting tricks can come only from trumps, so after cashing the jack of diamonds he plays a fourth round, which East ruffs with the nine. Declarer overruffs and when West wins with the ace of hearts he plays his fifth diamond, giving East a chance to ruff with the seven. South has to overtrump again and by this time West has established a second trump trick for himself.

Forcing dummy to ruff

When a defender has trumps which are open to a finesse by declarer he can sometimes ensure a trick by forcing the dummy to ruff, thus preventing a lead through his own trump holding. East has to be wide-awake to bring this about on the following hand:

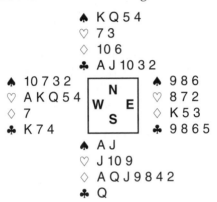

```
                  ♠ K Q 5 4
                  ♡ 7 3
                  ◊ 10 6
                  ♣ A J 10 3 2
   ♠ 10 7 3 2    ┌─────────┐   ♠ 9 8 6
   ♡ A K Q 5 4   │    N    │   ♡ 8 7 2
   ◊ 7           │  W   E  │   ◊ K 5 3
   ♣ K 7 4       │    S    │   ♣ 9 8 6 5
                 └─────────┘
                  ♠ A J
                  ♡ J 10 9
                  ◊ A Q J 9 8 4 2
                  ♣ Q
```

The bidding has gone:

South	West	North	East
1◊	1♡	2♣	Pass
3◊	Pass	3♠	Pass
4◊	Pass	5◊	All Pass

West leads the king of hearts and East has an opportunity for a clever piece of tactical misdirection. It is likely (since South has avoided Three No-Trumps) that partner holds all the top hearts; if dummy can be forced to ruff the third round, East can break the contract. So on the lead of the king of hearts East begins a mendacious peter with the seven; West continues with three rounds of hearts and East makes his king of diamonds. Even if East did not peter in hearts it would be good play for West to continue the suit; there is little hope of a trick from spades or clubs, so West should prefer the heart continuation to any other lead.

Making sure of a trump trick

The effectiveness of a plain suit lead through declarer, when the defender on the left can overtrump, is well known. In the following hand West makes a spectacular discard to bring this situation about.

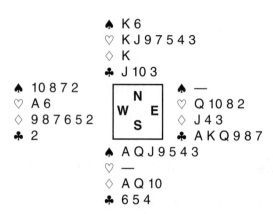

♠ K 6
♡ K J 9 7 5 4 3
◇ K
♣ J 10 3

♠ 10 8 7 2
♡ A 6
◇ 9 8 7 6 5 2
♣ 2

♠ —
♡ Q 10 8 2
◇ J 4 3
♣ A K Q 9 8 7

♠ A Q J 9 5 4 3
♡ —
◇ A Q 10
♣ 6 5 4

South plays in Four Spades after East has opened the bidding with One Club. West leads his singleton club, and when his partner wins the first lead with the queen it is obvious that the contract is on the way to defeat, unless – awful thought – South is void of hearts. But even this probability can be met. On the ace and king of clubs West discards first the three and then the ace of hearts; then a heart lead from East establishes a sure trump trick for the defence.

6

Partnership and Tactics
in Defence

Although there have been many changes in bidding since the early days of contract bridge, conventions in play have altered very little. The most important advances have been the development of suit-preference signals. The best known and the most valuable use of a suit-preference occurs when a player who has won a trick with such a holding as A-9-5-3-2 returns the suit for partner to ruff. He leads back the nine if he has a quick re-entry in the higher valued suit other than trumps, the two if he has a quick re-entry in the lower valued suit other than trumps.

Suit-preference signal at no-trumps

The convention is not limited to suit contracts, as the following example shows:

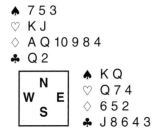

♠ 7 5 3
♡ K J
◇ A Q 10 9 8 4
♣ Q 2

♠ K Q
♡ Q 7 4
◇ 6 5 2
♣ J 8 6 4 3

The bidding has gone:

South	North
—	1◇
2NT	3◇
3NT	Pass

West leads the four of spades, East holds the trick with the queen and plays the king, on which South drops the nine and West the ten. East should be able to read the situation. His partner has led from A-10-8-4-2 and has played the ten on the second round to show that his re-entry is in the higher valued suit, hearts. So to the third trick East leads a heart and not a club.

Suit preference on the opening lead

A suit-preference signal can often be made on the opening lead. Suppose that you hold in hearts a six-card suit headed by A-K, and that you are defending a high contract by the opponents such as Five Diamonds. You have a void in spades and naturally want to put your partner in to give you a ruff. You are afraid that if you lead the king of hearts it is unlikely that the suit will stand up for two rounds; so you underlead the A-K, hoping that partner has the queen and will give you a ruff. As you want to ruff spades, your opening lead is a high heart such as the nine; if your void had been in clubs you would have led your lowest heart.

Two signals in one hand

Just as a player can make a suit-preference signal on the opening lead, so he can on the second lead. In the following example West makes two signals in the same suit.

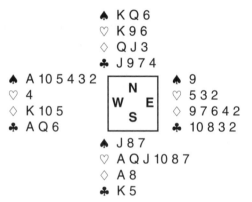

♠ K Q 6
♡ K 9 6
◇ Q J 3
♣ J 9 7 4

♠ A 10 5 4 3 2   ♠ 9
♡ 4   ♡ 5 3 2
◇ K 10 5   ◇ 9 7 6 4 2
♣ A Q 6   ♣ 10 8 3 2

♠ J 8 7
♡ A Q J 10 8 7
◇ A 8
♣ K 5

The hand was played in Four Hearts, and West, who had bid spades, opened with the ace and followed with the two. He was hoping that his partner could ruff and he led the two to show that his re-entry was in the lower valued suit, clubs. East could read the two of spades as a suit-preference signal, for West had bid spades and the two could not be his fourth best. So East ruffed and led back the two of clubs, showing a four-card suit. West won with the queen and, realising that declarer had the singleton king left, played the ten of spades to ask for a diamond return before the ace of clubs was knocked out. This defence put South three down and left him with only his honours as consolation for the thought that Three No-Trumps would have been a better contract.

A signal in the opponents' suit

Opportunities sometimes arise for a suit-preference signal in a suit which has been led by the opponents.

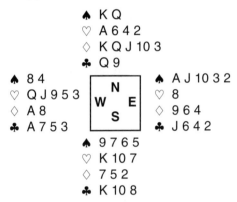

```
              ♠ K Q
              ♡ A 6 4 2
              ◇ K Q J 10 3
              ♣ Q 9
  ♠ 8 4           N          ♠ A J 10 3 2
  ♡ Q J 9 5 3   W   E        ♡ 8
  ◇ A 8           S          ◇ 9 6 4
  ♣ A 7 5 3                  ♣ J 6 4 2
              ♠ 9 7 6 5
              ♡ K 10 7
              ◇ 7 5 2
              ♣ K 10 8
```

The hand was played by South in Two No-Trumps, and the queen of hearts was led. South won with the king in his own hand and led a diamond. West played the ace at once and East dropped the nine. West decided that this must be an urgent call for a switch to spades; had his partner been satisfied with a heart continuation he would not have made this play of the nine of diamonds. So West led the eight of spades and East allowed dummy's queen to hold the trick. Declarer could run only seven tricks, and as soon as clubs were led West stepped in with the ace and led his second spade, setting the contract with four tricks in spades and two minor-suit aces.

A suit-preference signal can be valuable when one defender has to follow to a long suit led out by declarer and the other defender has to make some early discards. By discarding downwards, the player who has to follow suit can show that he controls one of the higher valued suits; in this way he may help his partner to find the best discards.

Signalling at the first trick

A debatable point is whether the convention should be employed on the first trick in defence to a suit contract. It often happens that the opening lead is king from A-K, dummy has a singleton, and third player has a holding such as Q-9-6-2. Some players drop the nine as a signal to show that they want a switch to the higher valued of the other two suits. However, this is a very dangerous practice to follow, for it often happens that the defender wants the suit to be continued, either to force the dummy or because any switch looks dangerous. If a high card is to be read as a suit-preference signal, then it becomes impossible to ask partner to continue the suit which he has opened. For this reason many players make it a rule that a card played to the first trick by the defender over dummy is suit-preference only in the clearest instance. With a long suit a player can have it both ways. From Q-J-10-8-5-2, for example, the eight on partner's king would be encouragement, the jack, an exaggerated signal, would be suit-preference.

The peter with three trumps

Most players know of the convention whereby a peter in the trump suit shows that the player had three trumps to start with. With 7-5-2 of trumps a defender plays the five and then the two to show he has a third trump. Opinions differ among good players as to whether this peter should always be made by a defender who holds three trumps, or whether it should be made only when he has a special reason for indicating to his partner that he holds a third trump.

The advantage of using the peter on all occasions is that it helps partner to count the hand. The advantage of petering only when the third trump is important – for example, when the player can ruff – is that the defenders sometimes gain a valuable clue to the best line of play.

To some extent it is possible to combine the advantages of both policies. The sensible solution is to make it a regular practice to peter with three trumps and to refrain from doing so only when you want to partner not to attempt to give you a ruff with your third trump.

When to peter with an honour

The general practice is to peter with J-x and 10-x, but not with Q-x. The play of the queen on partner's lead of the king shows that the jack is held as well. This information is often important, for it tells partner that if necessary he can underlead his ace.

3 D

```
                  ♠ Q 3
                  ♡ K 10 8 6 5
                  ◇ 7 4
                  ♣ 10 8 5 2
  ♠ J 9 5 4      ┌─────────┐     ♠ K 10 8 7
  ♡ J 4 3        │    N    │     ♡ Q 9 7
  ◇ Q 9 6        │ W     E │     ◇ 8 2
  ♣ A K 6        │    S    │     ♣ Q J 9 3
                 └─────────┘
                  ♠ A 6 2
                  ♡ A 2
                  ◇ A K J 10 5 3
                  ♣ 7 4
```

South plays in Three Diamonds and West leads the king of clubs, on which East plays the queen. Both defenders can see that to beat the contract they must take tricks in spades. As he cannot play trumps himself West leads a low club to the second trick and East returns a diamond. Declarer cannot ruff a spade without letting East into the lead again, so the defence win two tricks in spades, two in clubs, and one in diamonds.

The play from three small cards

There is some difference of opinion concerning the correct play on the second round by a player who has led the top card from a holding such as 8-5-2. The American practice is to vary the ordinary convention of play by dropping the five on the second round. Most British players would drop the two. In some situations the American convention helps partner, in others the British; it depends upon the size of the missing card held by declarer. This is as broad as it is long, so there is not really any good reason to depart from the ordinary convention of playing the low card. The difficulty of distinguishing between a lead from three cards and the lead from a doubleton is one that often causes trouble in defence. Many tournament players lead the middle card from three small and follow with the highest - a method known as MUD (Middle, Up, Down).

Shutting out dummy's suit

The rest of this chapter deals with tactical plays which centre round the trump suit. There are several situations in which defenders can save the game by refusing to overtrump. Here is one of them:

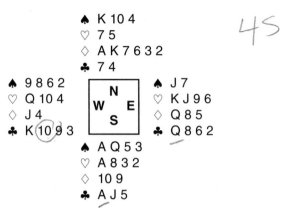

♠ K 10 4
♡ 7 5
◇ A K 7 6 3 2
♣ 7 4

♠ 9 8 6 2   ♠ J 7
♡ Q 10 4   ♡ K J 9 6
◇ J 4   ◇ Q 8 5
♣ K 10 9 3   ♣ Q 8 6 2

♠ A Q 5 3
♡ A 8 3 2
◇ 10 9
♣ A J 5

South plays in Four Spades and the ten of clubs is led, East playing the queen. South wins with the ace and the natural way to set about the hand is to play three rounds of diamonds, ruffing low on the third round. If West overruffs, declarer makes game without difficulty. West should see that if he holds on to his four trumps he can prevent dummy's established diamonds from becoming tricks. So on the third diamond West discards a club. Declarer can succeed now only by the unnatural play of leading the ace of spades and overtaking the queen on the next round.

✗ Adjusting the tempo

Most players know that it is a mistake on the part of a defender to ruff with a master trump in a position like this:

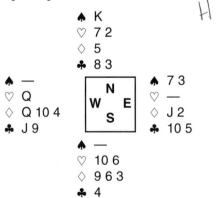

♠ K
♡ 7 2
◇ 5
♣ 8 3

♠ —   ♠ 7 3
♡ Q   ♡ —
◇ Q 10 4   ◇ J 2
♣ J 9   ♣ 10 5

♠ —
♡ 10 6
◇ 9 6 3
♣ 4

Hearts are trumps and declarer needs four of the last six tricks. The king of spades is led from dummy, South discarding a club. Now, course, it would be a bad mistake on West's part to ruff with the master trump. West should discard a diamond and when he wins the lead he can draw two trumps for one.

There are many extensions to this principle of not ruffing when it is possible later on to draw two trumps for one. The defender's mistake in the following hand often goes unnoticed:

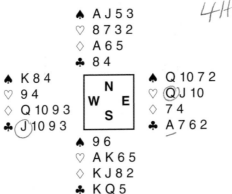

The jack of clubs was led against Four Hearts. East won with the ace and returned the queen of trumps. South thought he could see the way home for the loss of one club, one heart and one spade, so he drew two trumps, discarded a diamond in dummy on the top clubs, and followed with ace, king and a small diamond. East overtrumped with the jack, but there was still a trump in dummy to deal with the fourth diamond, so South made his game. The play seemed ordinary, but in fact both sides went wrong. As the play went, East should have refused to overtrump the third diamond. South cannot get out of dummy without letting East into the lead, and the play of the jack of hearts would then have drawn two trumps for one and left declarer with a losing diamond. However, South should not have given the defence this chance. He should have established communication between the two hands by ducking an early round of spades; East could then play a second trump but would never have the opportunity to lead the third.

Defence against declarer's two-suiter

In the last example the defender had to avoid an overruff in order to prevent declarer from making his trumps separately. There is one position, rather difficult to recognise, in which, by refusing to overruff, a defender causes declarer to lose control.

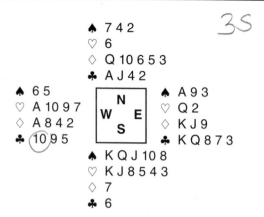

3S

The contract was Three Spades and West opened the ten of clubs. The play appeared to follow a normal course. Declarer won with the ace of clubs and finessed the jack of hearts; a trump lead at this point would have done no good, so West continued with another club. Declarer ruffed the club, ruffed a low heart and led a spade from the table, winning in his own hand. Another low heart was led, dummy ruffed and East overruffed. East played a high club, declarer ruffed, and as the last two spades were divided the rest of South's hand was high except for the losing diamond. The contract was made for the loss of two tricks in trumps, one in hearts, and one in diamonds.

The position when declarer led the third round of hearts was as follows:

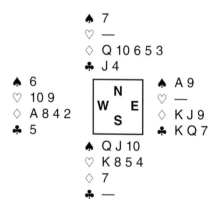

South had shown a marked two-suiter in the course of the bidding, and when the small heart was trumped in dummy East should have been able to work out that if he overruffed the contract would certainly be made. The right defence was to leave declarer in dummy so that to come back to his hand he would have to force himself once more.

See what happens if East discards a club instead of overruffing the heart. Dummy wins and leads a club, ruffed by declarer. If South leads a trump,

East wins and continues the force by leading a low diamond. Declarer's best hope is to lead the king of hearts rather than a trump. East ruffs with the nine of spades and refrains from playing the ace; instead, East leads a club or a low diamond and declarer loses control of trumps; if he continues to play hearts he allows West to make his small trump. The hand is a striking example of defensive tactics against a two-suited hand when trump control is in the balance.

Conceding a ruff and discard

There is another unusual way of upsetting the trump position when declarer has a long side suit; this is by conceding a ruff and discard and so preventing declarer from establishing his side suit.

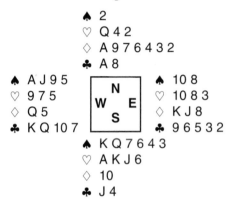

```
                ♠ 2
                ♡ Q 4 2
                ◇ A 9 7 6 4 3 2
                ♣ A 8
  ♠ A J 9 5         N          ♠ 10 8
  ♡ 9 7 5                      ♡ 10 8 3
  ◇ Q 5       W       E        ◇ K J 8
  ♣ K Q 10 7        S          ♣ 9 6 5 3 2
                ♠ K Q 7 6 4 3
                ♡ A K J 6
                ◇ 10
                ♣ J 4
```

The hand was played in Four Hearts and the king of clubs was led. Dummy won and a spade was lost to West's ace. West cashed the queen of clubs, on which South's jack fell. Ninety-nine players out of a hundred would lead a trump at this point, with some idea of preventing declarer from ruffing spades in dummy. The play then continues as follows: South wins in his own hand, ruffs a spade, then overtakes a trump return and plays a third round of trumps. As the trumps break 3-3 he can then afford to give up a spade. Had the trumps been 4-2 declarer would still have been all right if the spades had been 3-3; he needs an even break in one of the major suits and not worse than 4-2 in the other. The position would be the same if West played a diamond instead of a trump at trick four.

The reasoning that points to the right lead after the queen of clubs is quite simple. Obviously declarer is going to ruff spades in dummy, so why not let him trump a club instead? The difference is that ruffing a club in dummy does not help him to establish his spade suit. Study the effect of another club lead. If declarer trumps in dummy he must come back to his hand with a second trump and then ruff a spade with dummy's last trump. Declarer has to play ace and another diamond to get back to hand and then has to stake everything on a 3-3 break in both major suits.

The same position arises if declarer ruffs the awkward club in his own hand. He ruffs a spade in dummy, but has then no alternative but to take three rounds of trumps and hope that the spades will break as well.

Ruff and discard for an extra trump trick

Because to concede a ruff and discard is known to be bad play in the majority of situations, most players avoid it at all times. We saw in the last example that to concede a ruff and discard can be very effective play when declarer is obviously about to ruff a side suit in the dummy. A ruff and discard is never any good to declarer when he has no loser in the side suits, and sometimes a defender can come to an extra trump trick by forcing declarer to weaken his combined holding.

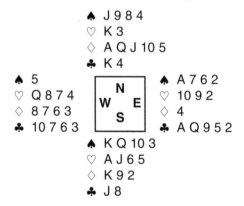

♠ J 9 8 4
♥ K 3
♦ A Q J 10 5
♣ K 4

♠ 5
♥ Q 8 7 4
♦ 8 7 6 3
♣ 10 7 6 3

♠ A 7 6 2
♥ 10 9 2
♦ 4
♣ A Q 9 5 2

♠ K Q 10 3
♥ A J 6 5
♦ K 9 2
♣ J 8

The contract is Four Spades and East wins the first two tricks with the ace and queen of clubs. It should be clear to East that the setting tricks can come only from the trump suit, so the best defence is to play clubs and concede a useless ruff and discard. Declarer's best play is to discard a diamond and ruff in dummy. When trumps are led East, of course, holds up his ace on the first two rounds; that is elementary. When South finds that East has four spades he will abandon trump leads, but as East can ruff the second round of diamonds South cannot possibly make the contract.

Ruff and discard in the endgame

Another time when it pays to allow a ruff and discard is when the alternative is to open up a suit which declarer hardly has time to establish himself.

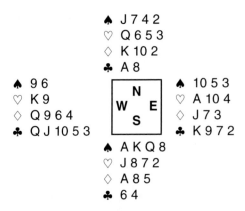

This hand was played in Three Spades and the queen of clubs was led. Declarer won in dummy and drew three rounds of trumps. Hoping to persuade the opponents to open up hearts, South followed with three rounds of diamonds. East won the third round and returned the two of clubs; this was good play, for it showed West that his partner held four clubs originally and gave him a chance to count the hand. The position when West won the second round of clubs was as follows:

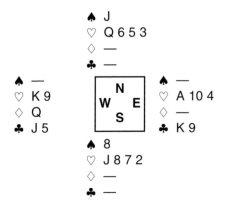

At this point West threw the hand away by leading king and nine of hearts. He knew that a diamond or a club would allow a ruff and discard and did not think further. If he had counted South's hand he would have known that South had four hearts, so that one ruff and discard would not help him much. A club should have been led, which South would have ruffed in his own hand; a heart is led, won by the king, and West plays the queen of diamonds, ruffed in dummy. East throws his losing heart on this lead and makes the last two tricks with the ace of hearts and a good club.

Declarer's play was not the best. He should have broached hearts himself after drawing trumps.

Conceding two ruff and discards

The phobia about conceding a ruff-and-discard is so prevalent, and so seldom referred to in bridge literature, that a fourth example is worth giving which shows a hand defeated only if this 'crime' is committed twice:

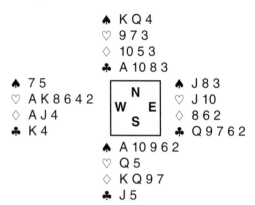

```
                    ♠ K Q 4
                    ♡ 9 7 3
                    ◇ 10 5 3
                    ♣ A 10 8 3
  ♠ 7 5                           ♠ J 8 3
  ♡ A K 8 6 4 2         N         ♡ J 10
  ◇ A J 4           W       E     ◇ 8 6 2
  ♣ K 4                 S         ♣ Q 9 7 6 2
                    ♠ A 10 9 6 2
                    ♡ Q 5
                    ◇ K Q 9 7
                    ♣ J 5
```

After some keen matchpoint bidding South became declarer in Three Spades. The defenders started with three rounds of hearts, East ruffing the third round and South overruffing. The trumps were drawn in two rounds and then declarer led a small club; West played low and declarer, thinking it likely that West was short in clubs, made the clever play of winning with dummy's ace and returning a club. This was the position:

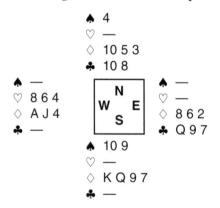

```
                    ♠ 4
                    ♡ —
                    ◇ 10 5 3
                    ♣ 10 8
  ♠ —                             ♠ —
  ♡ 8 6 4               N         ♡ —
  ◇ A J 4           W       E     ◇ 8 6 2
  ♣ —                   S         ♣ Q 9 7
                    ♠ 10 9
                    ♡ —
                    ◇ K Q 9 7
                    ♣ —
```

As he saw that a heart would allow a ruff and discard, West led a small diamond; the ten won and another diamond was led, establishing the suit; so declarer lost only one more trick. Study the effect of a heart lead by West. If dummy trumps, West allows the queen of diamonds to hold the next trick and makes his ace and jack. So declarer's best play is to discard a diamond from dummy and ruff in his own hand. South follows with the king of diamonds, which West ducks, and another diamond, which is won by the jack. At this point West gives declarer another chance for a ruff and discard, leading a further heart; declarer can ruff in either hand but still has to lose the last trick.

One last example, in which the ruff and discard applied the finishing touch:

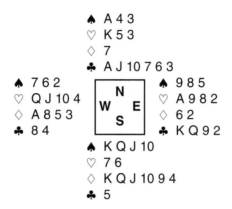

```
              ♠ A 4 3
              ♡ K 5 3
              ◇ 7
              ♣ A J 10 7 6 3
  ♠ 7 6 2                      ♠ 9 8 5
  ♡ Q J 10 4      N           ♡ A 9 8 2
  ◇ A 8 5 3    W     E        ◇ 6 2
  ♣ 8 4           S            ♣ K Q 9 2
              ♠ K Q J 10
              ♡ 7 6
              ◇ K Q J 10 9 4
              ♣ 5
```

The defenders led hearts against Four Spades and declarer had to ruff the third round. The king of diamonds was led and West played low! To have played the ace would have surrendered all chance of beating the hand. South continued diamonds, West ducked again, and a third diamond was ruffed by East. There was only one defence now, and East found it: a fourth heart and, turn and twist as he might, South had to lose another trick.

PART THREE
TACTICAL STROKES IN
THE MIDDLE GAME

7

Safety Plays

Safety play, properly so called, risks the loss of a trick which can be spared as an insurance against the possible loss of an extra trick which cannot be spared. For example, with this combination

Q 8 6 4

A 10 9 7 5 2

the right play from hand if declarer can afford to lose one trick is to play small away from the ace. This play may cost a trick if an opponent has the singleton king; but it is a safety play against the loss of two tricks should either opponent hold K-J-x.

By an extension of meaning many plays are described as safety plays which do not, in fact, risk the loss of a trick but are made as a precaution against a particular distribution. So in this position:

Q 8 6 4

A J 9 7 3 2

the lead of the queen is called a safety play because it takes into account the possibility that East may have K-10-5; if a small card is led for the finesse, East is left with K-10 over dummy's queen.

Technique in finessing

The last example is an exception to the general rule that a low card should be led when a finesse is about to be attempted. Some players would go wrong with a combination like this:

A Q 10 2

K 8   9 7 6 4

J 5 3

It is apparent that here the lead of the jack costs a trick.

The same situation arises in a different form in this example:

A J 10 7 5 2

9 4

An incautious lead of the nine costs a trick if West has a singleton honour.

An exception to the rule of leading low to a finesse was given in the second example in this chapter. The following position is of a similar kind:

A Q 8 6 3

J 7 5 2

If declarer needs all the tricks in this suit his best chance is to lead low and finesse the queen. But if his objective is to lose not more than one trick he should lead the jack - safety play against a possible holding of K-10-9-4 by West.

The same play appears in this diagram:

K J 8 4

Q 7 6 5 2

If East has the four outstanding cards nothing can be done about it but if West has them, the lead of the queen holds him to one trick.

Refusing finesses

There are many safety plays which consist of the play of top cards in preference to a finesse. Look at this very common position:

A Q 7 4

8 6 5 3

Although in the play of an actual hand it is often convenient to finesse, if there were nothing else to be considered the ace should played on the first round. This is simply a safety play to guard against the possibility of the player on your right holding the singleton king.

When there are nine cards in the two hands, safety play is important with this combination:

A Q 9 8 5

7 6 4 2

The best chance of making all the tricks lies in the finesse of the queen. But if declarer can afford to lose one trick he should play the ace first, for the finesse may lose to a singleton king.

This last example is well known; quite experienced players miss the right play in this position:

A Q 8 7 5 4

J 2

One trick must be lost however the cards lie, and the right play is the ace first. Players tend to lead small from dummy towards the jack; this is all right if East has the singleton king, but it loses two tricks when West has the singleton king.

The next diagram presents one of the most familiar combinations in the game:

K J 7 3

A 8 4

If four tricks are needed, of course the only hope is to play West for Q-x-x. Quite often declarer finds that he needs only three tricks from the suit. Then he must avoid the finesse; the ace and king are played and then a small card towards the jack; three tricks are made except when East has Q-10-x-x. The advantage of the safety play is that it takes into account the possibility that East may have Q-x; then, if a finesse is tried, East makes the queen and West wins the fourth round.

Deep finesses

The characteristic of the safety plays in the last group was that they protected high cards from losing to the high cards of an opponent. The next set of examples shows the use of safety play to prevent high cards from beating thin air. All players of any experience are familiar with this position:

K 5 3

A 10 7 4 2

The king is played from dummy and then a small card, East playing small; of course the ten is played in case East has Q-J-x-x. The same type of play is made with this holding:

K 9 5 4

A 10 7 6 2

If the declarer can afford to lose one trick in the suit the safety play is to lead the two, and if West plays the three, to put on the four from dummy. This line of play ensures four tricks whichever opponent holds Q-J-8-3.

With this combination:

K 9

A 10 7 5 3

the best chance of making four tricks is to lead low and finesse the nine; if West started with Q-x or J-x, the defenders are held to one trick.

Playing for the best chance

There are several combinations in which the choice between lines of play is very close. The best play with this holding:

K 9 6

A 10 8 4

may vary according to whether West or East is likely to have length. When there is no indication, to play off the ace and king is as good as anything. This loses two tricks only if one opponent has Q-J-x-x.

It is fairly well known that with this combination:

A 9 8 5

Q 10 7 3

The best chance is to take two finesses. The ten is led and run, and if it loses to the jack a second finesse is taken against the king. This play loses two tricks only if East has both king and jack.

The play is different when nine cards are held between the two hands:

A 9 8 5 2

Q 10 6 4

If two finesses are taken, two tricks are lost when East has K-J-x and also when he has K-J alone. The best play to make four tricks is to lay down the ace. This loses two tricks if West has K-J x, but not if West has K-J alone;

therefore, it is better play than taking two finesses. If entries permit, there is a correct way of playing the following combination:

Q J 7 4

K 8 3

The usual play is to lead small to the jack and then play back to the king, making three tricks only if the opposing cards are divided 3-3. It is possible to take advantage of the extra chance that West has the ace once guarded. The best play is to lead towards the Q-J and, if this holds the trick, to return to hand and lead low again from K-x. If West had originally A-x the defenders are held to one trick, and declarer still makes three tricks when the original distribution was 3-3.

Avoiding the loss of two tricks

There is a group of safety plays in which the player's object is to limit his losses to two tricks. Safety play almost always lies in refusal to take a finesse on the first round.

A Q 7

10 8 6 4 2

If declarer can afford to lose two tricks the right play is to play the ace and later to lead low towards Q-7. This safety play is proof against any 4-1 distribution.

The same play is made if the five cards are headed by the A-Q:

A Q 8 5 2

10 6 4

To avoid the loss of three tricks the safety play is to lay down the ace and then lead small towards the 10-6.

The play is the same if the queen and ten are interchanged:

A 10 5

Q 8 7 4 2

Again declarer can afford to lose two tricks, but not three. The ace should be played first and later a small card towards the 10-5. This safety play is fool-proof against any 4-1 distribution.

Some special safety plays

A few combinations present special safety plays which cannot be classified under any of the headings above.

K J 7

A 9 6 4 2

There is only one sure way of making four tricks against any distribution. The king is played first and later a small card towards J-7. The play succeeds whichever opponent has Q-10-x-x.

A rather different play is made if the jack and nine are interchanged:

K 9 5

A J 7 4 2

To make sure of four tricks, play ace and then a small card towards the K-9. If West follows suit, cover whatever card he plays; if West shows out, go up with the king and lead back towards the jack. Most players know how to tackle this combination:

10 7 4

A K 8 6 3

Declarer plays the ace, and if West plays queen, jack, or nine, the safety play to make four tricks is to lead low towards the 10-7. The correct play with the following combination is not so well known:

A 9 7 5 3 2

J 6

There is only one chance of losing only one trick. This is to lead low from dummy and play East for K-10 or Q-10.

There are some safety plays which have little practical importance. You might play for a lifetime before you could reap the benefit of knowing the safety play with this combination:

10 7

A Q 8 6 5 4 2

To make sure that you do not lose more than two tricks, the play is to lead low away from the ace.

The examples of safety plays so far have centred round the play of a single suit. Many of these safety plays have their counterpart in the larger field of strategy.

Protecting a master card

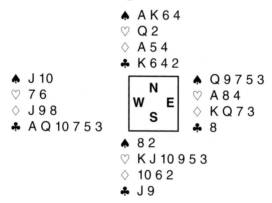

```
                    ♠ A K 6 4
                    ♡ Q 2
                    ◇ A 5 4
                    ♣ K 6 4 2
 ♠ J 10                              ♠ Q 9 7 5 3
 ♡ 7 6            N                  ♡ A 8 4
 ◇ J 9 8       W     E               ◇ K Q 7 3
 ♣ A Q 10 7 5 3    S                 ♣ 8
                    ♠ 8 2
                    ♡ K J 10 9 5 3
                    ◇ 10 6 2
                    ♣ J 9
```

The contract is Three Hearts by South, the opponents not having bid. The jack of spades is led and dummy wins. East wins the first or second round of trumps and leads his singleton club, West winning with the ace and returning the queen. If declarer automatically puts on the king from dummy, that card is ruffed and there are no discards for the two losing diamonds. The correct safety play is to allow the queen of clubs to hold; the next round can be ruffed, and the king of clubs can be used later on for the discard of a diamond.

A more difficult example of the same sort of play, in which a card is protected from an enemy ruff, is seen in the following hand:

```
          ♠ 6 5
          ♡ Q J 9
          ◇ 7 6 3 2
          ♣ A 8 7 4
             N
          W     E
             S
          ♠ A K 4 3 2
          ♡ A K 10 8 4 3
          ◇ A
          ♣ 5
```

The contract is Six Hearts and a diamond is led. It looks as though declarer has a reasonable play for Seven Hearts, but if he is careless he may go down in Six. Suppose he starts off with the ace and king of spades. If either opponent has a singleton spade, he will ruff and no doubt lead a trump. The effect of this will be that South has three losing spades left in his hand and only two trumps in dummy, so that the contract will go one down. There is an attractive safety play to make sure of the contract. Declarer should play the ace of spades and then a low spade from each hand. If spades are divided 5-1, declarer has now only two losers and cannot be prevented from ruffing them both.

Safety play is called for on any number of hands when the contract is in sight without risk, provided that declarer counts his tricks. In rubber bridge most players would go wrong on this hand:

Nine tricks wanted

♠ J 8 5
♡ K 3
♢ A Q 10 5
♣ K Q J 4

```
        N
    W       E
        S
```

♠ K 10 3
♡ A J 2
♢ 8 7 4 3
♣ A 9 5

The contract is Three No-Trumps and West opens with the five of hearts, East's queen falling to the ace. If declarer counts his tricks he will see that there are eight on top. If he attempts to develop the ninth by playing on diamonds he may find that East has K-J-9-x and that the setting tricks are established in hearts before the vital ninth trick can be made. Diamonds look tempting, but the way to make sure of the ninth trick is to attack spades. The king is led to the second trick, and after this declarer cannot fail against any lie of the cards.

The next hand is another example of the use of a safety play in preference to a finesse:

Finding the extra tricks

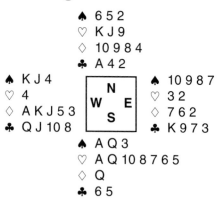

```
                ♠ 6 5 2
                ♡ K J 9
                ◇ 10 9 8 4
                ♣ A 4 2
   ♠ K J 4         N        ♠ 10 9 8 7
   ♡ 4          W     E     ♡ 3 2
   ◇ A K J 5 3     S        ◇ 7 6 2
   ♣ Q J 10 8              ♣ K 9 7 3
                ♠ A Q 3
                ♡ A Q 10 8 7 6 5
                ◇ Q
                ♣ 6 5
```

West opens with One Diamond and North/South end up in Four Hearts. West leads the king of diamonds and his natural continuation is the queen of clubs. South can make a certainty of the hand if he plays correctly. He must win with the ace of clubs and lead the ten of diamonds, discarding a club from his own hand. Whatever West plays, the trumps are drawn and the two losing spades are thrown on the nine and eight of diamonds, which between them are worth one trick. So declarer discards three losers on the 10-9-8 of diamonds, but makes sure of one trick. Note that if the club led at the second trick is not won at once in dummy, East can overtake with the king and return a spade, giving declarer no chance to recover.

Chapters 2 and 3 contained a number of examples of safety plays whose object was to ensure the establishment of tricks in a side suit. The characteristic of those plays was that declarer was protecting himself against possible loss of trump control. There are many safety plays made to take care of a side suit when there is no danger of losing control. Often declarer has to make sure of a ruff in dummy.

Making sure of a ruff

```
        ♠ A Q 6
        ♡ 7 4
        ◇ 9 8 4 2
        ♣ Q 7 5 3

        N
      W   E
        S

        ♠ K J 8 7 5
        ♡ K 8 6
        ◇ A K 3
        ♣ A J
```

The contract is Four Spades and the eight of clubs is led; East plays low and South wins with the jack. Only carelessness can lose him the contract. If he enters dummy with a high trump in order to lead towards king of hearts, the defenders have a chance to draw all dummy's trumps before any hearts can be ruffed; then declarer may lose three tricks in hearts and one in diamonds. Of course the right play is to make sure of the ruff in hearts whatever the distribution. Declarer can afford to lose two tricks in hearts and should play a small heart from his own hand at the second trick. The defence then has no time to draw trumps before the all-important heart ruff has been obtained.

Players sometimes hesitate to open up rather shaky-looking side suits before trumps have been drawn. They have a vague idea that they are running the risk of a ruff which should be prevented.

Prompt attention

```
        ♠ K J 5
        ♡ 7 6 3
        ◇ K 10 3
        ♣ A 6 5 3

        N
      W   E
        S

        ♠ 8 7 3 2
        ♡ A 4
        ◇ A Q J 4 2
        ♣ 7 2
```

The contract is Three Diamonds and the opening lead is won by the ace of hearts. South can count seven top tricks and requires two tricks from spades. It would be a mistake to draw trumps before setting about the spades. It is true that an early spade lead exposes declarer to the danger of a ruff if the suit is badly distributed, but if that happens nothing would have been gained by postponing spade leads. Suppose, for example, that East has Q-x and that he wins an early finesse in spades, returns the suit to his partner's ace, and ruffs the third round. Declarer loses three tricks in spades, but so he would have done had he drawn trumps immediately.

Suppose, on the other hand, that East's spade holding is A-x. Then an early finesse of the jack fetches the ace and declarer makes one trick with the king and one by ruffing the fourth round of the suit. Had he drawn trumps immediately, the defenders would have held him to one trick in spades and the contract would have been defeated.

There is one interesting situation in which what appears to be risky play is in fact safety play.

Taking care of a side suit

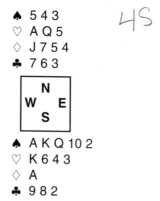

```
          ♠ 5 4 3
          ♡ A Q 5
          ◇ J 7 5 4
          ♣ 7 6 3
              N
          W       E
              S
          ♠ A K Q 10 2
          ♡ K 6 4 3
          ◇ A
          ♣ 9 8 2
```

The contract is Four Spades and the enemy start off with three tricks in clubs, followed by a diamond. Assuming that the trumps break, declarer has to avoid the loss of a heart. Most players would play out all the trumps and hope that if the hearts were divided 4-2 the defenders might make a mistake. A better hope is that if the hearts are 4-2, the hand which has four hearts has also three trumps. The correct play, therefore, is to play two rounds of trumps and then three top hearts; if one of these is ruffed, the contract cannot be made by any play (unless a rather unlikely squeeze develops in the red suits); if both opponents follow to three rounds, the last heart is good and the outstanding trump can be drawn. It may happen that the player who started with a doubleton heart had also only a doubleton in trumps; then the third round of hearts will stand up, the fourth round can be ruffed, and the lead regained for the last trump to be drawn.

The same play appears in a less obvious guise in the next example:

♠ 6 5 4
♡ A 7 3
♢ J 8 5 4
♣ A 4 2

♠ A K Q J 7
♡ K 8 5 2
♢ A
♣ 6 5 3

The contract is again Four Spades and a club is led; declarer wins the second round and his next play should be to duck a round of hearts. His only worry on the hand is the fourth heart; after taking an early round he intends to play two rounds of trumps when he regains the lead and then the ace and king of hearts, hoping, as before, that if the suit breaks 4-2, the player with the four hearts has also three trumps and will be helpless when the last round is ruffed in dummy.

It is not easy to see at once why a round of hearts has to be ducked so early in the hand. The reason is that if declarer plays ace, king and a small heart at once, West may win and play a fourth round on which East can overruff the dummy. Alternatively, if declarer plays two rounds of trumps before ducking a heart, the player who wins the heart trick may play a third trump, so preventing any chance of a ruff by dummy.

There are many opportunities for safety play in the handling of a cross-ruff. An example was given in Chapter 3 of the importance of establishing tricks in a side suit before embarking on a cross-ruff. It often happens that towards the end of a hand a player can see his contract on a cross-ruff provided that he is not overruffed; sometimes he can ensure against this possibility by ruffing with master cards, and this he should always do if he sees that he can afford it.

A high cross-ruff

♠ Q 9 3
♡ K J 6 5 4
◇ A K 7 3 2
♣ —

♠ A K 10 4
♡ 7
◇ 4
♣ A 9 8 7 5 4 2

North/South reach the only game contract which has much chance of success, namely Four Spades. West makes things easier by the lead of ace and another heart, dummy's king holding the trick. Declarer should sum up his chances as follows: there are four tricks to be made in the side suits, so six are needed from trumps; the trump tricks are certain so long as he can ruff low once in each hand, as after that he can afford to ruff high and still make a trick out of the ten and nine. The ace and king of diamonds are cashed and a diamond is ruffed (a diamond being led for the ruff rather than the heart, as West would have preferred the lead of a doubleton diamond, if he had it, to the ace of hearts, which might be from A-x). Then the ace of clubs is played and a club ruffed low in dummy; if all these cards stand up, the position is:

♠ Q 9
♡ J 6 5
◇ 7
♣ —

♠ A K 10
♡ —
◇ —
♣ 9 8 7

Having made four tricks in the side suits, and two by ruffing, South requires four more tricks. It is at this point that the safety play is made. He should ruff the next three tricks with the ace, king and queen spades, and then he is assured of one trick through the ten and nine; if the safety play is not made, there may be an overruff by the jack, and a trump continuation will beat the contract.

A more spectacular and in some ways rather simpler example of the same type of play is seen in the next hand:

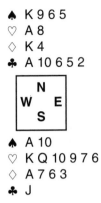

```
          ♠  K 9 6 5
          ♡  A 8
          ◇  K 4
          ♣  A 10 6 5 2
              N
          W       E
              S
          ♠  A 10
          ♡  K Q 10 9 7 6
          ◇  A 7 6 3
          ♣  J
```

A diamond is led against Six Hearts. The safest line of play is to ruff the third round of diamonds with the ace of hearts and the fourth round with the eight, losing at most a trick in trumps. If the third round of diamonds is ruffed low, East may overruff and return a trump; and if declarer plays trumps right away and the trumps do not break, he will probably have to lose a diamond as well as a heart.

Conceding an early trump trick

Every player has met hands which are easy so long as dummy's side suit can be brought in. The solution to these hands is sometimes to give up an early and possibly unnecessary trick in the trump suit.

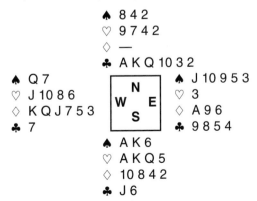

```
                    ♠  8 4 2
                    ♡  9 7 4 2
                    ◇  —
                    ♣  A K Q 10 3 2
  ♠  Q 7                              ♠  J 10 9 5 3
  ♡  J 10 8 6            N            ♡  3
  ◇  K Q J 7 5 3     W       E        ◇  A 9 6
  ♣  7                   S            ♣  9 8 5 4
                    ♠  A K 6
                    ♡  A K Q 5
                    ◇  10 8 4 2
                    ♣  J 6
```

The contract is Six Hearts and the king of diamonds is led. Declarer ruffs in dummy and the right continuation is to duck a round of hearts immediately. It is not difficult to see that if declarer plays out his high trumps West will interrupt the play of the clubs and declarer will be left with losing diamonds.

The need for the same type of play is perhaps more difficult to see in the next example:

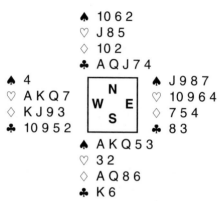

```
              ♠ 10 6 2
              ♡ J 8 5
              ◇ 10 2
              ♣ A Q J 7 4
  ♠ 4              N          ♠ J 9 8 7
  ♡ A K Q 7    W       E      ♡ 10 9 6 4
  ◇ K J 9 3        S          ◇ 7 5 4
  ♣ 10 9 5 2                  ♣ 8 3
              ♠ A K Q 5 3
              ♡ 3 2
              ◇ A Q 8 6
              ♣ K 6
```

South plays in Four Spades after West has made a take-out double of One Spade. Three rounds of hearts are led, South ruffing the third round. The hand is straightforward if the trumps break, but in view of West's take-out double it is quite likely that East has the suit held. Declarer's problem is the same as before; if he leads out A-K-Q of trumps, East will interrupt the play of the clubs and declarer will lose a diamond in addition to two hearts and a spade. The safety play is to lead the ace of spades and follow with a small one; now a diamond return can be won with the ace, and a heart return can be dealt with by the dummy.

Had one of the top spades been in dummy, the play would have been rather more simple. Say that dummy had A-x-x and declarer originally K-Q-x-x; then the K-Q of spades could be led and the clubs run off until East ruffed.

8
Communication Plays

The plays that are made to stop the opponents going from hand to hand, or to help one's own side to do so, are among the most brilliant and difficult in the game. It is a characteristic of these entry-making and entry-killing plays that they are available equally to the attacking and defending sides; for the mechanics of play are the same whichever side plays the dummy.

The commonest of all communication plays is the hold-up. Some examples of hold-up play were given in Chapter 2. There are times when hold-up play is a mistake; by going up at once with a high card, declarer (or it may be a defender) can block the run of an enemy suit.

Blocking plays

This is quite a common position:

A 6

3 led

10 9 5 4

If declarer plays low, East may win with an honour and clear the suit. If West had originally a five-card suit headed by two honours, four tricks are established for the defence. By going up with the ace on the first lead, declarer can prevent the opponents from running four tricks. If the suit is divided 4-3 it makes no difference whether he plays high or low, and in any event the opponents take only three tricks. But if West has five cards headed by two honours, then the play of the ace blocks the suit and, if the opponents have only one quick entry, they cannot run four tricks. It is, of course, most unlikely that West would have led low from a suit headed by K-Q-J.

Exactly the same play is made with this combination:

A J

9 8 6 5

By playing the ace on the opening lead you can prevent the run of the suit if East has two cards headed by an honour.

Whether it is better to hold up or to try to block the enemy often depends on which opponent is likely to obtain the lead first:

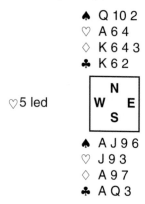

♠ Q 10 2
♡ A 6 4
◇ K 6 4 3
♣ K 6 2

♡5 led

♠ A J 9 6
♡ J 9 3
◇ A 9 7
♣ A Q 3

The danger in Three No-Trumps is that West's lead of the five of hearts may be from a five-card suit and that he may have an entry in the king of spades. Since the contract is safe if East has the spade king, nothing can be gained by hold-up play. It is, however, quite possible that East has K-x or Q-x of hearts. If so, the play of the ace of hearts at the first trick will block the run of the suit. It is true that East may have 10-x and West have led from K-Q-x-x-x; but this is a lesser chance than the other.

The next hand is a less obvious example of the same type of play:

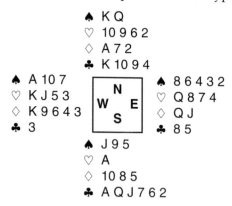

♠ K Q
♡ 10 9 6 2
◇ A 7 2
♣ K 10 9 4

♠ A 10 7
♡ K J 5 3
◇ K 9 6 4 3
♣ 3

♠ 8 6 4 3 2
♡ Q 8 7 4
◇ Q J
♣ 8 5

♠ J 9 5
♡ A
◇ 10 8 5
♣ A Q J 7 6 2

South was declarer in Five Clubs after West had made a take-out double on the first round. West led the four of diamonds and the fate of the hand depends on declarer's play to the first trick. The ordinary play in this sort of situation is to hold up for one round in the hope that the player who wins with the ace of spades will not have a third diamond to lead. On this occasion there is little hope of such play succeeding. As West has made a take-out double he is sure to hold the spade ace and no doubt he has length in diamonds. There is one chance, and that is that East holds two honours in diamonds. If so, the run of the suit can be blocked by putting up the ace from dummy. As the cards lie, this play comes off. Trumps are drawn and spades led; West wins and cannot run two tricks in diamonds; the jack of spades affords a discard for dummy's diamond.

Declarer quite often has the chance to block the run of an opposing suit when an opening lead has been made of a low card from three to an honour.

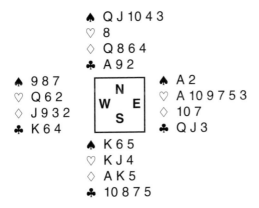

```
            ♠ Q J 10 4 3
            ♡ 8
            ◇ Q 8 6 4
            ♣ A 9 2
♠ 9 8 7                      ♠ A 2
♡ Q 6 2          N           ♡ A 10 9 7 5 3
◇ J 9 3 2    W       E       ◇ 10 7
♣ K 6 4          S           ♣ Q J 3
            ♠ K 6 5
            ♡ K J 4
            ◇ A K 5
            ♣ 10 8 7 5
```

This was the bidding:

South	West	North	East
—	—	—	1♡
Pass	1NT	Pass	2♡
Pass	Pass	2♠	Pass
3NT	All Pass		

West led the two of hearts – correct, of course, on his holding of three to an honour. East won with the ace and returned the ten. Now if South finesses the jack the hand is easily defeated. South should be able to read the position; as West did not support hearts on the first round and as East rebid the suit, the distribution is surely 6-3 and West has led from Q-x-x. If this is right the play of the king at the second trick will block the run of the suit.

Second hand high

There are many positions in which the play of a high card by the second player interrupts the enemy communications.

A J 9 6 4

K 10 2   Q 7 5

8 3

Imagine that there are no side entries to the dummy and that South leads a low card. If West plays low the nine is finessed, and if East wins with the queen declarer can make four tricks; if East holds up the queen declarer makes an extra trick with the nine. The correct defence is for West to play the king; then, if there are no other entries to the dummy, South is held to one trick.

This type of play is needed to defeat the contract of Three No-Trumps on the following hand:

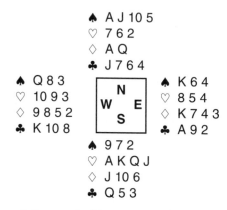

♠ A J 10 5
♡ 7 6 2
◇ A Q
♣ J 7 6 4

♠ Q 8 3   ♠ K 6 4
♡ 10 9 3   ♡ 8 5 4
◇ 9 8 5 2   ◇ K 7 4 3
♣ K 10 8   ♣ A 9 2

♠ 9 7 2
♡ A K Q J
◇ J 10 6
♣ Q 5 3

West led the two of diamonds, East won and returned his fourth best. In dummy at the third trick declarer entered his hand with a heart and led a low spade. To beat the hand, West must go up with the queen of spades. If West plays low, the ten is finessed; East may hold up, but declarer can make three tricks in spades by ducking the next round. After the play of the queen declarer can make only two tricks in spades; if dummy wins with the ace, East, of course, will hold up the king on the next round of the suit.

The play of an unnecessarily high card by the second player makes the defence much easier on the next hand:

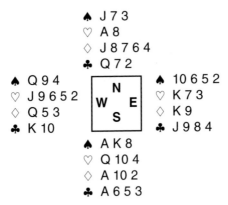

West led the five of hearts against Three No-Trumps, East won with the king and played a heart back. Declarer played a small diamond from dummy and this was the critical moment. If East plays low, South finesses the ten, West wins and clears the hearts; on the next round of diamonds the king falls and South makes game with two spades, two hearts, four diamonds and one club. East can defeat the contract by playing the king of diamonds on the first lead of the suit; South wins and plays the ten of diamonds, but West naturally holds off; when he wins the third round he clears his heart suit and gets in with the king of clubs to make his last two hearts.

It is true that even if East fails to put up the king of diamonds West can save the situation by refusing to put his queen on the ten; but this is a difficult play, for West cannot read the position for certain and may be giving up a vital trick. The play of the king of diamonds by East is clearly marked and can hardly lose since in any case this card must fall on the next round. There are many other combinations in which the play of a high card from a doubleton may have an unexpected result, as in the diagram which follows:

A J 10 7 6 4

K 5   Q 9 2

8 3

On the lead of the eight West should play the king. It is true that East can prevent the establishment of the suit by not winning the first trick if West plays low and the ten is finessed, but there is no reason why West should leave his partner to make the decision. Furthermore, the play of the king may result in the defenders winning two tricks. If South is not an experienced player he may decide that his best chance is to play West for K-Q-x; then he will allow West to hold the trick with the king and on the next round he may finesse and lose to East's queen.

A Q 10 8 6 4

K 7   J 9 3

5 2

Here again West should play the king on the first round, especially if the situation is such that declarer wants to establish dummy's suit without letting West into the lead.

A difficult and seldom recognised play occurs in this position:

K 9 8 7 6 5

J 10 4   A 3

Q 2

Imagine that the lead is in dummy and that dummy has one side entry which can be quickly attacked. A small card is led, and if East plays low declarer wins with the queen and of course ducks in dummy on the next round. East can prevent the suit from being established by playing the ace on the first lead and attacking dummy's entry before South's queen has been played off.

It was remarked at the beginning of this chapter that the various entry-killing plays were available equally to attackers and defenders. In the next example the play of second hand high has to be made by declarer; if he misses it, the defenders can beat the contract with the help of an unblocking play.

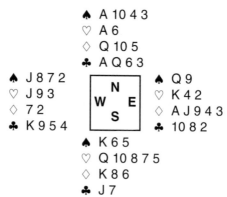

♠ A 10 4 3
♡ A 6
◇ Q 10 5
♣ A Q 6 3

♠ J 8 7 2   ♠ Q 9
♡ J 9 3   ♡ K 4 2
◇ 7 2   ◇ A J 9 4 3
♣ K 9 5 4   ♣ 10 8 2

♠ K 6 5
♡ Q 10 8 7 5
◇ K 8 6
♣ J 7

South played in Three No-Trumps after East had made an overcall of One Diamond. A small diamond was led and declarer played low from dummy. East finessed the nine and declarer won with the king. A heart was led to the ace and East correctly unblocked the king. After that, declarer could not establish hearts without letting West into the lead, and another diamond from West set up four tricks in the suit. Declarer could have prevented the establishing of diamond tricks by playing the queen on the first lead; then the defenders would have been helpless.

The Deschapelles coup

When the attack on dummy's entry card is made at the cost of a trick, the play is known as the Deschapelles coup. This coup is generally shown in the form of a spectacular lead of an unsupported king made in order to drive out dummy's ace. In the following example the right play is perhaps more difficult to find.

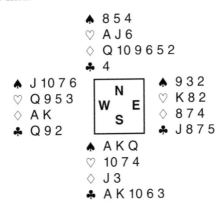

West leads the six of spades against Three No-Trumps. Declarer wins and leads the jack of diamonds. Now it should be obvious to West that he must attack dummy's ace of hearts before his own second stopper in diamonds has been knocked out. The play to the opening lead has shown that South has all the spade honours, so the hand cannot be defeated by continuing spades. It is not good enough to lead the three of hearts or even the nine; West must play the queen; this forces the ace and later on East can prevent the jack from becoming an entry.

The Scissors coup

One way of preventing the opponents from going from hand to is to lead early on the suit in which their only line of communications exists. This far-seeing play is known as the Scissors coup.

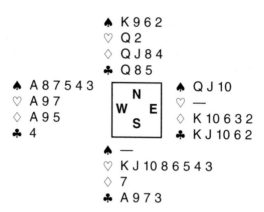

After competitive bidding South became declarer in Five Hearts doubled. The singleton club was led, dummy played low and the ten forced the ace. A heart was led to the queen, on which East played the six of diamonds, and a second heart was taken by the ace. West underled his ace of diamonds to put his partner in with the king, and a low club was led and ruffed by West. The declarer still had to lose the ace of diamonds and two more tricks in clubs, so he was three down, losing three clubs, a heart and a diamond.

Despite this good defence declarer had a chance to save one trick. When he won with the queen of hearts in dummy he should have played the king of spades, discarding the singleton diamond from his own hand. West would then have been unable to put his partner in with the lead of a low diamond and declarer would have made a trick at the finish with the nine of clubs.

The coup was more clearly marked when the following hand was played:

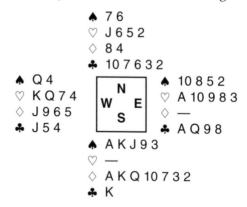

After some adventurous bidding South played in Five Diamonds doubled. The king of hearts was led and ruffed, and before drawing trumps declarer rightly explored the spade suit. He led ace and king of spades, and when the queen fell it was apparent that only one spade ruff would be needed, so he led out the ace of diamonds, on which East discarded a heart. A low spade followed, West ruffing with the nine of diamonds; West then led a club, won by East, and East smartly returned the fourth spade, setting up a trump trick for West's jack. South thought he had been unlucky, but it was easy to foresee that this would happen and South could have prevented it by leading a club after the ace of diamonds; then West after winning with the nine of diamonds would not have been able to put his partner on lead.

The Scissors coup can sometimes be countered by means of unblocking play on the part of the defence.

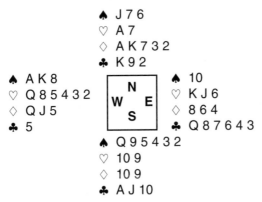

The hand was played in Four Spades, doubled by West. West led his singleton club, declarer won and played a low spade. West took the king and switched to hearts. Declarer won in dummy and led the jack of spades; West won with the ace, put his partner in with a heart, and was given a club ruff to set the contract.

When declarer was in with the ace of hearts he should have tried to bring off the Scissors coup by playing ace, king and another diamond, discarding the heart from his own hand; if this trick is won by West he cannot put his partner in the lead for a club ruff. However, a perfect counter is open to the defence in the form of a double unblock by West with the queen and jack of diamonds; this defeats the declarer's attempt to cut the communications between the defending hands.

Creating entries for partner

The best-known method of creating entries to partner's hand is exit play. Exit play is, of course, very common in the defence to elimination and throw-in play. Sometimes the Deschapelles coup, generally used to drive out dummy's entries, is used to create an entry to partner's hand:

```
                    A 7
        Q 9 6 5 3          K 8 2
                    J 10 4
```

Imagine that West has an established side suit but has no apparent entry card. By leading the king of spades East forces an entry to his partner's hand.

A spectacular way of setting up an entry for partner is to throw away a master card in one's own hand. The following hand is a standard example:

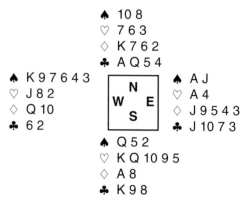

```
                  ♠  10 8
                  ♡  7 6 3
                  ◇  K 7 6 2
                  ♣  A Q 5 4
   ♠ K 9 7 6 4 3      ┌─────┐      ♠ A J
   ♡ J 8 2            │  N  │      ♡ A 4
   ◇ Q 10          W  │     │  E   ◇ J 9 5 4 3
   ♣ 6 2              │  S  │      ♣ J 10 7 3
                      └─────┘
                  ♠  Q 5 2
                  ♡  K Q 10 9 5
                  ◇  A 8
                  ♣  K 9 8
```

South plays in Three No-Trumps after a spade lead by West. West overtakes the jack of spades at trick two and forces out the queen; on this trick East discards the ace of hearts. Then declarer cannot establish hearts without allowing West into the lead, and he has no play for the contract. There is an important group of plays in which the defenders maintain communications by not releasing their high cards on the first lead of a suit. Study the following problem from East's point of view:

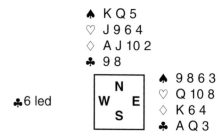

```
                  ♠  K Q 5
                  ♡  J 9 6 4
                  ◇  A J 10 2
                  ♣  9 8
                      ┌─────┐      ♠ 9 8 6 3
                      │  N  │      ♡ Q 10 8
        ♣6 led     W  │     │  E   ◇ K 6 4
                      │  S  │      ♣ A Q 3
                      └─────┘
```

South has opened One No-Trump vulnerable and North has raised to Three No-Trumps. The question is: which club should East play to the first trick?

It is evident from the Rule of Eleven that South holds only one card higher than the six; this card is surely the king, in view of South's vulnerable no-trump bid. The strength of the dummy and of East's hand is such that it is clear to East that West has no side entry. If, therefore, East goes up with the ace, South will hold off until the third round and the suit will never be brought in. But if East plays the queen South will not dare to hold up the king, lest the ace be on his left. When East obtains the lead with the king of diamonds he will be able to play the ace and a small club, allowing his partner to run the suit. Had East's holding in clubs been A-J-x or A-10-x, the jack or ten would equally have been the correct play.

The play of the middle card by East is generally right when the position is as follows:

$$2$$
$$\text{A 9 7 6 3} \qquad\qquad \text{K J 4}$$
$$\text{Q 10 8 5}$$

Assume this time that West has a quick entry. If East plays the king to the opening lead and returns the jack, South will cover, and since West has the entry card the suit cannot be brought in by the defence. If, on the other hand, East plays the jack on the first trick, it makes no difference whether South holds off or not. Probably South will win, and when West obtains the lead later on he can lead low to his partner's king. For this defence to succeed West must, of course, be familiar with the stratagem used by East and must realise that his partner may have the king.

There is one other play in this group which is very rarely brought off:

$$\text{6 4 2}$$
$$\text{A 10 8 7 3} \qquad\qquad \text{K J}$$
$$\text{Q 9 5}$$

West leads the seven and East, if he judges that West is unlikely to have a side entry, should play the jack. If East plays the king and returns the jack, South will play low; but if the jack is played on the first trick South is certain to win, and later on East will play the king and West will overtake to run the suit

Creating an entry to dummy

The commonest of all manoeuvres to maintain communication with partner's suit is the familiar ducking play. This is so well known that there is no need to give examples, except to remark in passing that safety occasionally calls for ducking play at unexpected moments. For example, with A-K-J-8 6 4 2 in dummy and 7 3 in his own hand, it may be right for declarer, if he can afford one loser and has no other entry to dummy, to duck the first round in case West has Q-10-9-5. An entry to dummy is sometimes forced by sacrificing a trick in one suit in order to gain tricks in another. Every now and again declarer finds himself with such a holding in trumps as A-K-Q-J-10-9-6-2 in his own hand and 7-5 in dummy. If dummy has two side winners which cannot otherwise be reached, it may be good policy to give up a trump trick to the opponent's eight, so that a certain entry is gained to dummy.

Stealing base

Entry to partner's hand is quite often won in defence by means of an underlead. The clever stratagem brought off by West on the following hand is worth noting:

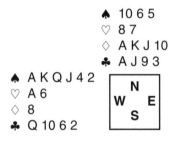

```
            ♠ 10 6 5
            ♡ 8 7
            ◇ A K J 10
            ♣ A J 9 3
♠ A K Q J 4 2    ┌─────────┐
♡ A 6            │    N    │
◇ 8             │ W     E │
♣ Q 10 6 2      │    S    │
                └─────────┘
```

In the course of the bidding South showed at least a six-card heart suit and North/South bid to Four Hearts. West led his singleton diamond, hoping, when he won with the ace of trumps, to put his partner in the lead with the ten of spades for a diamond ruff. However, the ten of spades turned up in dummy. The king of diamonds won the first trick, East playing the two; a heart was then played and West won with the ace. It seemed impossible to defeat the hand, for declarer was marked with five tricks in hearts, four in diamonds (in view of East's two) and one in clubs. But there was just a chance that East held the nine of spades and that a low spade from West would catch declarer napping; so West, when he won with the ace of hearts coolly led a low spade; South, who held a singleton spade, did not think of playing the ten from dummy, and when East recovered from his surprise at winning the trick with the nine he returned a diamond to defeat the contract.

Establishing an entry for one's own suit

The next hand shows a way of preserving an important entry card.

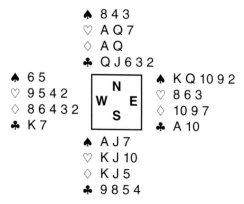

After East has made an overcall of One Spade South becomes declarer in Three No-Trumps. West leads the six of spades, and the fate of the hand is decided by East's play to the first trick. If he plays the queen South ducks, and as East has only one more entry the spades are never established. But if East plays the nine on the first trick the hand is defeated, for West wins the first lead of clubs and has a second spade to lead while East still holds the ace of clubs.

The following hand is a more complicated example of this type of play:

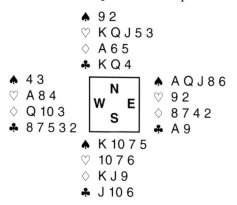

Again the contract is Three No-Trumps and West leads four of spades. If East makes the natural-looking play of the jack, South can make the contract by playing low. But if East plays a low spade at the first trick the hand is defeated, assuming that declarer plays first on the heart suit. When West wins with the ace of hearts he has a spade to lead; East clears the suit and comes in later with the ace of clubs.

The defender's play on the next hand has the same strategical object: he ducks the first lead so that his partner may retain small cards in the suit.

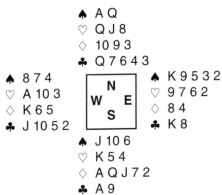

West leads the eight of spades against Three No-Trumps and the queen is played from dummy. East must not release the king on the first lead; if he does, the hand cannot be defeated. East should play the nine of spades; then when West wins with the king of diamonds he will play a second spade, and when in with the ace of hearts a third spade; at this point East's king will come into its own.

Keeping one player out of the lead

A declarer often wants to establish a suit without letting a particular opponent into the lead. To accomplish this, some unusual plays may be needed. Suppose a suit is distributed like this:

$$A Q 10 7 4$$
$$K 8 5 \qquad\qquad J 9 3$$
$$6 2$$

If he plays correctly South can set up four tricks without allowing East to obtain the lead. If the queen is finessed and the ace laid down, West can unblock with the king. To prevent this, South should return to his own hand for the second lead; if West plays the king he is allowed to hold the trick; otherwise the ace is played from dummy and West has to win the third round.

Declarer's play of the following hand accomplishes a similar object by different means.

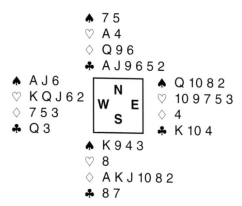

West led the king of hearts against a contract of Five Diamonds. Declarer's difficulty is that apparently he cannot establish clubs without allowing East into the lead to play a spade through the king. The solution is childishly simple once you think of it. The king of hearts is allowed to hold the trick. Then a club is discarded on the ace of hearts and the suit established without further loss.

Refusing to cover

The right play on the following hand is similarly unexpected:

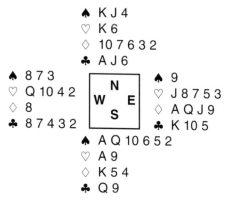

West led his singleton diamond against Four Spades. East won with the ace and returned the queen. South covered with the king and West ruffed and made the right switch to a club; from this point declarer could not avoid losing to the king of clubs and the jack of diamonds. An unusual safety play was needed to make sure of the contract. South should have refused to cover the queen of diamonds; West would have ruffed the third round but the fifth diamond could have been established for a club discard.

Leading dummy's suit

Declarer's communications with dummy can sometimes be severed by means of a direct attack on dummy's long suit. This defence sometimes has to be started with the opening lead; it is not an easy play, for the defenders may not, at first, be sure how many cards declarer has of dummy's long suit.

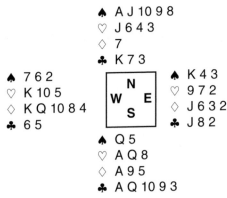

The king of diamonds was opened against Six Clubs. South won and took the spade finesse right away. East won with the king and led a trump, with some idea of preventing ruffs by dummy. However, only one ruff was needed and declarer made the slam without difficulty. A heart or diamond return by East would have been equally innocuous. The only successful defence is a spade return. To bring in dummy's spades South has then to draw three rounds of clubs, finishing in dummy. The spades are run off, but as he had not been able to ruff a diamond South has to take the heart finesse for his twelfth trick. It is an instructive hand, for not many players in East's position would appreciate the strength of a spade return at the third trick.

9

Deceptive Plays

There are a few spectacular bluffs; and a host of minor deceptions in which the right choice of card leaves the opponents in doubt. When you hold cards of equal rank such as K-Q, or of insignificant rank such as 7-4-2, you know that in defence it matters a good deal which one you play, as every card says something to partner. Playing the dummy you have no partner to inform, but you have two opponents to misinform, and in most situations there is a right and a wrong card for declarer just as there is for a defender.

The choice of card

This is a simple example:

```
                    6 4 2
        5 led                     J played
                    K Q 7
```

If at no-trumps you win this lead with the queen, West will know that you have the king as well; so you should win with the king and leave West to wonder about the queen. Most players would do the right thing here; but make the position a little more complicated, and the best play is not so easy to see.

```
                    6 4 2
        7 led                     J played
                    A K 3
```

At no-trumps you may decide to hold off the first trick; then you should win the second round with the ace, and East may not realise that you have the king as well. But suppose you think that another suit looks more dangerous and so decide to win the opening lead. Which card do you think is better, the ace or the king? In fact the king is better, because to play the ace on the first round at no-trumps is 'give-away' that the king is behind it.

Low cards can be just as important as high ones. This is a situation:

```
                    Q 9 3
        A K J 8 7                1 0 6 4
                    5 2
```

West has bid this suit and he leads the king against a trump contract. You drop the five; West, missing the two, may think that his partner has started a peter and may continue the suit to your advantage.

Many players false-card from habit, making no distinction between one situation and another.

```
                    Q 8 5 3
        A K J 9 7                4
                    1 0 6 2
```

As before, West has bid the suit and leads the king against a trump contract. You can read East's four as a singleton. Now it would be foolish to play the six or ten from your hand, for the only effect would be that West, missing the two, would be able to place his partner with either singleton or doubleton. Your best hope is to play the two and hope West reads you for the singleton.

In all these situations it gives the show away if you have to ponder over the card you are going to play. You can avoid being caught napping if you remember this: as declarer put out the same signals as you would if you were defending: play a high card if you want a suit to be led, a low one if you hope to stop it.

```
                    A K J
        10 led
                    Q 7 5 2
```

When West leads this suit against you at no-trumps you want to give him the impression that he has found your weakness. Play the king from dummy and cover whichever card East plays. If East plays the three or four, you play the five; if East plays the six or eight, you play the seven. Of course your object is to make West think that East is signalling. When you open up a suit yourself you can often do it in such a way that the opponents may misread your holding.

```
                    A Q J 3

                    K 6 2
```

You have this combination at no-trumps, and you may think that there is not much to the way you play it. But there can be. You may be able to give West the impression that his partner holds the king, and later in the hand this may tell in your favour.

Your first play in the suit should be to lead the six from your hand and play the jack from dummy. Of course it is unfair to look at East with an air of anxious expectancy; but equally you should avoid playing the jack in such a way that it is obvious to both opponents that you know it will hold. By concealing the two you may lead West to conclude that his partner is holding up the king and is putting forth a mild signal. After this trick you play another suit from dummy. It is not at all easy, by the way, to cultivate a manner of playing high cards in such a style that there is no indication whether or not you expect them to hold the trick. If you watch carefully, you will find that you can generally tell whether a player is taking a finesse or playing a winner.

Come into my parlour

There are several ways of inducing opponents to continue a suit to your advantage.

<pre>
                    8 4
      Q 9 7 5 3   10 6 2
                    A K J
</pre>

You are declarer at no-trumps and West leads the five. It may be that there is another suit which you fear much more, and that you can go game if the opponents do not switch to this other suit at the first opportunity; so you win the first lead with the king, not the jack.

<pre>
                    J 10 3
      K 8 6 4 2   7 5
                    A Q 9
</pre>

West leads fourth best and you play the jack from dummy. It is good shot to play the queen from your own hand; West may play you for A-Q alone.

<pre>
                    J 9 3
      A Q 8 7 5 2   4
                    K 10 6
</pre>

This is the same play in slightly different form. West leads the seven, you play the jack from dummy and the ten from your own hand; when West gets in, he may be tempted to lay down the ace.

If an opponent opens a suit which you had intended to develop yourself, you can generally win a further tempo if you are not too hasty.

<pre>
                    Q 10 6 5 3
      K 7   J 9 4
                    A 8 2
</pre>

At some point West leads the king, hoping to find his partner at home in the suit. Instead of winning with the ace and clearing the suit, giving the opponents a chance to attack elsewhere, you play the eight. Flushed with success, West will clear the suit for you.

```
                        8 3
        10 7 6 4                 Q 9
                     A K J 5 2
```

You are declarer at no-trumps and West leads a suit which you have concealed in the bidding. When the queen is played by East, drop the five; East is sure to continue and you gain a tempo.

Defenders have rather fewer opportunities for this sort of stratagem. Sometimes when holding A-Q over dummy's K-J-10 it is a good move to win the ten with the ace, tempting declarer to take a second finesse in this suit rather than to play for tricks in another suit; or it may happen that declarer will become careless and take a second finesse when he has his contract safe.

This is an attractive manoeuvre:

```
                     Q 10 9 4
        7                        A K J 6 3
                     8 5 2
```

At no-trumps declarer leads low and finesses the nine. East plays small and waits for declarer to repeat the performance.

False security

Curious effects can be obtained by not playing off winning cards. A defender who has the thirteenth of a suit often does better not to play it when he has a possible side winner, for if declarer has alternative plays he is sure to take a finesse into what he imagines is the 'safe' hand.

The following hand is a clever example of this type of play:

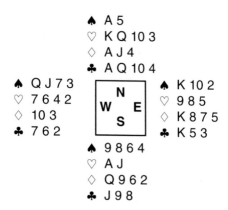

South played the hand in Three No-Trumps in a matchpointed contest. West led the three of spades, East won with the king and returned the ten: South entered his hand with a heart and took a club finesse. When East won with king of clubs he sized up the position as follows: 'Partner led the three of spades and I hold the two, so there are only two tricks to take in this suit. Prospects are poor, for declarer is obviously home with four tricks in hearts, three in clubs, one in diamonds and one in spades. There is only one chance. If I play back a club now, and not a spade, declarer may become overconfident and let me in with the king of diamonds: Let's give it a ride.

So East returned a club and South, thinking his position secure, saw no reason why he should not try the diamond finesse for a tenth trick. East won and produced the two of spades to defeat the contract. South's play was not so bad as it looks, for in a matchpoint game declarer is sometimes justified in taking a risk for an overtrick; at rubber bridge he is never justified in doing this - but he may do it all the same.

Making a defender guess

Second hand has an awkward guess in this familiar position:

           K 10 6 3

    Q 8 4

           J led

If the lead is from A-J-9, it is a mistake to cover; but if declarer's holding is J-x-x, the second player looks foolish if he does not cover. The lead of the jack from J-x-x opposite K-10-x-x is not technically correct, because it cannot gain against best defence; but because the defender may misread the position, the jack is a good deceptive lead when West is unlikely to hold a doubleton Q-x.

West is in a dilemma in this position:

```
                A 5
      K 8 4 3
                Q led
```

From West's point of view, it is likely that the queen is top of a sequence, so as a rule West will play low. You can take advantage of this every now and again at a suit contract by slipping through the queen from a holding such as Q-x-x.

With these cards you can play on the nerves of the right-hand defender:

```
                Q 9 8 5
      J 6 4               A 10 7 3
                K 2
```

At a suit contract you play small from dummy and win with the king. You enter dummy and lead another low card. You play the same way if you have K-J alone; East has to guess.

There is quite an art in making opponents crash their honours. With a holding such as Q-7-6-3 in dummy and J-10-8-5-4-2 in your own hand you should always try the lead of the queen from dummy.

Another position in which you can sometimes bring about a crash is this one:

```
                K 8 4
      J 5                A Q 7
                10 9 6 3 2
```

The suit is trumps and you lead low to the king, losing to the ace. Make the next lead from dummy; East is quite likely to play the queen.

This is a combination which has possibilities:

```
                7 4
      Q 3                A 10 6 5
                K J 9 8 2
```

This is a side suit in a trump contract. You play from dummy and win with the king. You lead from dummy again next time, just as you would if you had K-Q instead of K-J; East has to take a view. The basis of all these 'honour-crashing plays is that you lead from dummy towards the closed hand when you are missing the top controls.

Stealing tricks

Many tricks can be picked up by underleading at the right moment. The best moment of all is the opening lead.

```
           K 7 6 4 2
A Q J 9                10 8
           5 3
```

The opening lead of the queen through a suit bid by dummy will almost always hold the trick in this sort of position. The lead can also be tried when dummy has bid no-trumps and is marked with the king.

The underlead from A-K-x through Q-10-x is well known and wins more tricks than it deserves. Less frequently seen is this play:

```
           A J 7
K Q 5 4                10 8 3
           9 6 2
```

The lead of a small card by West will generally win an extra trick for the defence and risks nothing.

There are a few situations, not so well known, in which the defenders can conjure up a trick like magic.

```
           Q 10 7 2
A K 4                  J 8 3
           9 6 5
```

In a suit contract West leads the king and East peters with the eight. West follows with ace and a small one, and declarer is almost certain to finesse the ten, expecting East to ruff. There are several variations of this play.

```
           Q 9 6 4
A K 5 3                10 7 2
           J 8
```

East peters in the same way and declarer finesses the nine on the third round; the ten forces declarer to ruff and he cannot get a discard until the trumps have been drawn.

```
           10 6 4
J 8 2                  A Q 9 3
           K 7 5
```

If East plays this suit he should lead the queen. Declarer will probably play low, for he will think that East has Q-J-9. West can help things along by playing the eight, and on the next round East leads the three; declarer is quite likely to duck again.

A first cousin to this play is seen in this position:

10 6 4

A J 7 2   Q 9 3

K 8 5

Again East leads the queen; this time declarer has to make only one wrong guess. The same play can be made by the defence when the position is the other way up, with K-8-5 in dummy and Q-9 underneath it.

The following deception is well known but is still good for several tricks, because although the defender may suspect what is going on, he cannot be sure:

A Q 6 5

10 8 4   K 7 3 2

J 9

The bidding has marked East with the king, so declarer plays the ace from dummy and then a small card, as though intending to ruff; East has an awkward decision to make.

A more subtle version of this type of play is seen in the following deal:

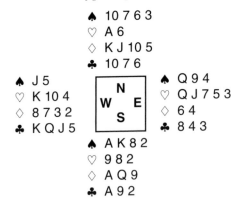

The contract is Four Spades and the king of clubs is led. As a matter of ordinary technique you hold off the first lead and win a second club with the ace. The play looks straightforward. You lay down ace and king of spades and then play to discard a club on the fourth diamond; the play comes off so long as the man with the third trump has at least three diamonds.

As the cards lie it appears that you fail, for East ruffs the third diamond and the defence can still make a club and a heart. Nevertheless, clever play gives you a good chance to land the contract. Instead of playing out ace, queen and a small diamond, you play the ace, small to the king and the ten back.

East is likely to think that if he ruffs with the queen he will be ruffing a loser with his master trump. If East lets the jack pass you return to dummy with the ace of hearts and discard the club loser on the last diamond.

False-carding in defence

There are a few situations in which a defender must false-card, a few in which he generally should, and many more in which he should vary his play about equally between true and false cards.

Some examples follow of what are known as 'obligatory' false cards:

A J 8 6 2
K 7   10 9 5
Q 4 3

Declarer leads a small card and finesses the jack. East must play the nine or ten, so that declarer will have alternative plays on the next round.

5
J 10 4   A 3
K Q 9 8 7 6 2

The singleton is led from dummy and South wins with the king or queen. West must drop the ten, for otherwise declarer cannot go wrong on the next round. After the ten has fallen declarer may lead an honour on the next round, playing West for J-10 alone.

The play in the next example is more spectacular but is quite well known:

A J 7 5 2
K 10   8 6 3
Q 9 4

On the lead of the four by declarer West plays the king; South is quite likely to place East with 10-8-6-3 and finesse the nine on the next round. A defender can try the same play with Q-10 sitting over J-9-5 when there is A-K-7-6-3 opposite.

Q 10 8 6 4
K 7 5 2   J 9
A 3

In this position the play of the jack by East on the first round is likely to induce a finesse of the eight on the next round. This is a coup which has many intricate variations.

The last two examples illustrate an important principle in defensive play, namely that if it does not sacrifice a trick a defender should always play a card which he is known to hold or which he will be known to hold after the next trick.

Playing the card which you are known to hold

```
                    K 9 6 3
        8 7 4                   Q 10 2
                    A J 5
```

Declarer finesses the jack and then lays down the ace. East must clearly play the queen, the card he is known to hold, so that South will have to decide whether to play for the drop or finesse the 9. Here is a very common situation:

```
                    6
        10 7 4                  K J 8 3
                    A Q 9 5 2
```

This is a side suit in a trump contract. Declarer finesses the queen and begins to ruff out the suit. East must play the king immediately, for until this card has been played declarer knows that dummy can ruff low with impunity.

In various positions it is good tactics to play a card which is bound to fall on the next round.

```
                    K 10 6 4
        Q 8                     J 9 5
                    A 7 3 2
```

When the ace is led West should drop the queen, especially if it is trumps. Fear that the trump suit is divided 4-1 may change declarer's whole plan.

The psychological factor

The examples in the last two sections have been of false cards which, generally speaking, should always be played. Of course there are innumerable positions in which a defender should sometimes play a false card and sometimes a true one. It is obvious that a player who always false-cards in certain stock positions (for example with doubleton Q-J) is easy to play against.

How you should play often depends on your estimate of declarer's intelligence.

$$A J 9 6 2$$

K 4   10 7 3

$$Q 8 5$$

Declarer leads the five and finesses the jack, reserving the decision whether to play West for K-x or East for 10-x. Against a fairly innocent player the seven is a good false card to play as East; it will incline declarer to play you for 10-7. But if declarer is experienced and knows that you are up to all the tricks, you do better to play the three. He may then work out that the one holding you are not likely to have is 10-7-3, for with that holding he would expect you to play the seven.

In the next example declarer's estimate of your partner also comes into the picture:

$$K 10 5 3$$

J 8 6 4   2

$$A Q 9 7$$

On the lead of the ace or queen the eight by West is a clever false card which can be recommended in most circumstances. The object, of course, is to persuade declarer to play you for the singleton rather than your partner. But if the standard of play is very high, South may be struck by the fact that East has played the two and may infer from this that East is unlikely to have J-6-4-2; so in an expert game it may be better for West to play the four and leave declarer an open guess.

A famous situation

If you are observant you can pick up a lot of extra tricks against defenders who do not vary their false cards. Study this very common position:

$$K J 8 6 2$$

Q 9 7   10 3

$$A 5 4$$

You play the ace and in the hope of putting you off the finesse East drops the ten. Except against a beginner you probably take no notice and still finesse the jack. Now look at it this way:

$$K J 8 6 2$$

10 9 7   Q 3

$$A 5 4$$

You lead the ace and this time East, the same inveterate falsecarder, plays the three. What can you infer? Why, that East has not got a plain doubleton, for with 10-3, 9-3, or 7-3, he always drops the higher card in this position. So you conclude that the finesse cannot be a winning play and accordingly go for the drop. If you can resist the temptation to comment on your acumen you can pick up thousands of points a year by close attention to details of this kind.

Heading them off

There are many opportunities for skilful play to put opponents off the scent when they appear to be hot on the trail of your weakness.

```
                    Q 10 7 4 3 2
        K 8                        J 9 5
                    A 6
```

At no-trumps declarer leads the ace. West can see the danger that the suit will be established on the next round, so he drops the king. South will probably look for other fields to conquer.

The same sort of play can be made by the right-hand defender:

```
                    A 6
        10 8 5                     K J 9
                    Q 7 4 3 2
```

The ace is led from dummy and East plays the king; disconcerting for South.

Declarer has an opportunity for striking play in this situation:

```
                    J 9 3
        4                          A Q 10 8 7 6
                    K 5 2
```

The suit has been bid on your right, so you can read the four as a singleton. To avert an immediate ruff you play the king under the ace and East will probably conclude that his partner has led the middle from three small.

The same play can be made against the left-hand opponent:

```
                    J 10 6 3
        A Q 9 7 5 2                8
                    K 4
```

West leads the ace of a suit which he has bid twice. If you see a chance of a future discard you can try dropping the king under the ace. It may not be easy for West to know what is going on.

Masking the weak suit

Every experienced player knows how effective can be the lead by declarer himself of the suit which he most fears. At no-trumps the best way of averting attack in a suit of which you hold something like 6-5-2 in dummy and J-10-4 in your own hand is to play it from dummy at the first opportunity.

Most players are less well versed in the art of simulating strength in a suit which an opponent has led.

Q 4

K played   5 led

10 7 3

A possible way to avert a continuation of the suit by West is gravely to 'unblock' with the queen from dummy. The same play can be made when dummy holds J-x or J-x-x, and if you want to be really clever you can try it with K-6 in this position:

K 6

A played   5 led

9 7 3

A well-judged discard

Every now and again an opportunity arises for the clever play which declarer made on the following hand.

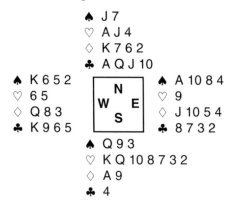

```
              ♠ J 7
              ♡ A J 4
              ◇ K 7 6 2
              ♣ A Q J 10
  ♠ K 6 5 2      N        ♠ A 10 8 4
  ♡ 6 5       W     E     ♡ 9
  ◇ Q 8 3        S        ◇ J 10 5 4
  ♣ K 9 6 5               ♣ 8 7 3 2
              ♠ Q 9 3
              ♡ K Q 10 8 7 3 2
              ◇ A 9
              ♣ 4
```

North/South bid to Six Hearts without stopping to enquire about aces, and in the play this turned out to their advantage. West led a heart, won in dummy, and South deliberately did not take a second round of trumps at once, for he did not want to give East a possible chance for an informative discard. At trick two he led the ace of clubs and then he ran the queen, discarding the nine of diamonds from his own hand. There is always a temptation for a defender to attack a suit which declarer is seen to be discarding, and West promptly switched to the queen of diamonds.

East missed a chance to make a suit-preference signal. On the second round of clubs he should have played the eight, to indicate strength in the higher valued suit, spades.

Note that after the trump lead, there is a pretty way to make the contract of Six Hearts by force. Declarer plays four rounds of diamonds (ruffing two in his hand) and all the trumps, reducing West to the king of spades and K-9-6 of clubs and dummy to the jack of spades and A-Q-J of clubs. Then a finesse of the jack of clubs is followed by the jack of spades. Whichever defender wins this trick must lead into a major tenace. This is the 'winkle squeeze'.

PART FOUR
THE ENDGAME

10

Throw-in Play

The term throw-in play' is generally used to describe the familiar position in which an opponent is forced to lead towards a tenace holding. In this position:

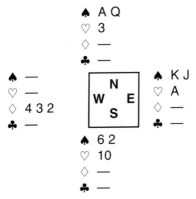

```
                    ♠ A Q
                    ♡ 3
                    ♢ —
                    ♣ —
   ♠ —                           ♠ K J
   ♡ —          ┌──────────┐     ♡ A
   ♢ 4 3 2      │    N     │     ♢ —
   ♣ —          │ W     E  │     ♣ —
                │    S     │
                └──────────┘
                    ♠ 6 2
                    ♡ 10
                    ♢ —
                    ♣ —
```

South accomplishes a throw-in by leading a heart and forcing East to lead into the spade tenace.

Although this type of endplay is easy to understand and is very common in play, it is in some ways less easy to execute than the other forms of endplay. The reason for this is that the player has to risk losing the lead at a critical moment and there are many ways in which the defenders can make things difficult. Declarer may bring off elimination play and even squeeze play without taking any risk and often without needing to study very carefully the holdings of the opponents. To bring off a throw-in, however, declarer must always have a good idea of what is going on.

Finesse and endplay

To make the maximum number of tricks on the following hand needs careful technique in finessing as well as an endplay:

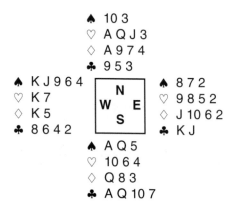

South plays in Three No-Trumps after West has made an overcall of One Spade. The opening lead of the six of spades is won by dummy's ten.

The honours in hearts and clubs lie so favourably that four tricks can be made in both suits so long as declarer does not make the mistake of leading a high card towards the finesse. A low club is led, the finesse holds, a low heart is led back, and so on until the following position is reached:

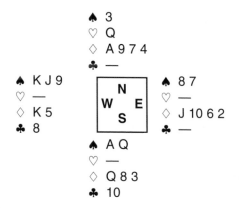

The lead is in dummy. Declarer plays the queen of hearts and then a spade to the ace. The ten of clubs is cashed and at this point West has three cards left; the natural cards for him to keep are the king of spades and K-5 of diamonds; remembering West's overcall of One Spade, South throws him in with the king and forces him to lead away from his king of diamonds. In this way twelve tricks are made.

West can, however, make the play more difficult by discarding in a less obvious manner. A good player would see what was coming; he would throw the five of diamonds early on and at the eleventh trick the jack of spades, keeping K-4 of spades and the king of diamonds alone. If declarer has not kept a careful watch of the cards played, he will go wrong at this point. Endplay can often be defeated if the defender can see ahead and unguard his honours.

Retaining an exit card

To bring off throw-in play declarer must have a card with which to exit. It often happens that ordinary hold-up play is declined for the sake of retaining a card with which to exit later in the hand:

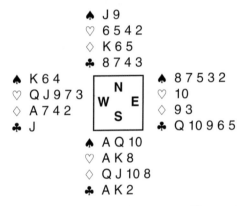

The contract is Three No-Trumps and the queen of hearts is led. South can see eight certain tricks after the ace of diamonds has been cleared. The only danger to the hand is that West may hold the ace of diamonds and king of spades together with long hearts.

Declarer can make certain of his contract so long as he avoids the risk of a spade finesse. The opening heart lead should be won and the ace of diamonds forced out. West plays another heart and declarer wins again. When dummy wins with the king of diamonds, declarer does not take a finesse in spades as he has a certain exit card with which to throw the lead. The diamonds are run off and the ace and king of clubs played. By this time South has a perfect count of West's hand. He exits with a heart at the ninth trick and West, after making two more tricks, has to lead away from the king of spades at trick twelve.

Throw-in with elimination

The various forms of endplay are often intermingled. In the next example declarer has to use the tactics of elimination play before effecting the throw-in.

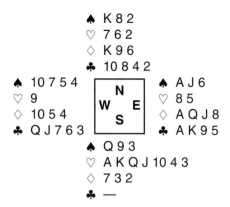

♠ K 8 2
♡ 7 6 2
◇ K 9 6
♣ 10 8 4 2

♠ 10 7 5 4
♡ 9
◇ 10 5 4
♣ Q J 7 6 3

♠ A J 6
♡ 8 5
◇ A Q J 8
♣ A K 9 5

♠ Q 9 3
♡ A K Q J 10 4 3
◇ 7 3 2
♣ —

South played in Four Hearts doubled after strong bidding by East. A club was led and ruffed high. After drawing the trumps South had nothing better to do than to lead a low diamond and finesse the nine, letting East win with the jack. East led a club, South ruffed and led a spade to the king; East won and played a third club, which South ruffed high. The position then was:

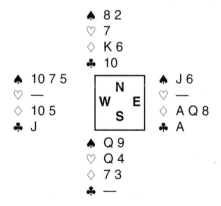

♠ 8 2
♡ 7
◇ K 6
♣ 10

♠ 10 7 5
♡ —
◇ 10 5
♣ J

♠ J 6
♡ —
◇ A Q 8
♣ A

♠ Q 9
♡ Q 4
◇ 7 3
♣ —

South laid down the queen of spades, to which East played low. Then a small heart was led to the seven and the last club led to eliminate East's clubs. South then threw the lead with the spade, and East had to lead a diamond at the twelfth trick.

South played the hand well to go only one down, but the defenders missed no fewer than three chances to avoid the endplay. Their first opportunity was when a low diamond was led to the fourth trick; West could have resolved all difficulties by playing the ten, but it must be admitted that this play might, from West's point of view, have turned out to be a mistake. The real culprit was East. When the queen of spades was led out, East should have realised that South was unlikely to have the Q-10 and if he had, an endplay was certain. Having failed to drop the jack of spades under the queen, East had another chance to disembarrass himself of this card when the low heart was led to dummy's seven; instead of throwing the diamond, he should have discarded the jack of spades.

The contract of Six Spades reached on the next hand could have been made by means of a squeeze against East; in practice it was made by a throw-in combined with elimination.

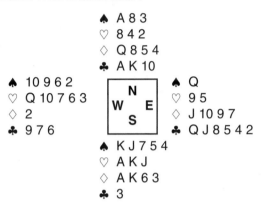

As the bidding had shown that North/South held all the aces, West led the nine of clubs rather than his singleton diamond. Declarer tackled trumps at once and discovered East's singleton. After winning three rounds of trumps South played the ace of diamonds and then a small diamond towards the queen, on which West discarded a heart. It would, of course, have been bad play for West to ruff. Dummy won with the queen of diamonds, leaving the position as follows:

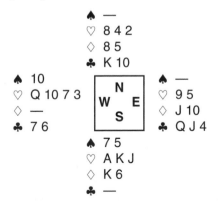

Declarer knew that West had started with four spades and a singleton diamond; there was a slight inference from the lead and from the subsequent play that West had not more than three clubs originally, so South continued by leading king and another club to eliminate West's clubs; then the last spade was led, forcing West to lead away from the queen of hearts.

The hand was played in a duplicate game, and at another table South made his contract by means of a squeeze against East. A trump trick was given up early on, and when declarer made all his winners in the major suits, East was squeezed in the minors.

Throw-in with a squeeze

The next hand has the character of squeeze play as well as of a throw-in:

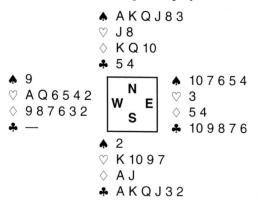

Good bidding arrived at the best contract of Six No-Trumps by South. A diamond was led and won by declarer. After a round of clubs had shown West's void, declarer tested spades; West again showed out after dropping the nine on the first round. Declarer could now place East with five cards of both black suits; furthermore there was a tenace position in spades. The way was clear for a throw-in. First the king and queen of diamonds were cashed, forcing East to part with three of hearts; then the top clubs were played out and East was thrown in with the last club to lead into the spade tenace.

The next hand is a combination of squeeze and throw-in with loser-on-loser play.

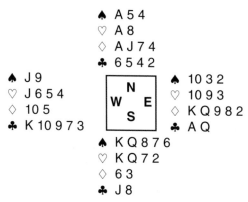

The contract was Four Spades. West led a club and East won with the ace and returned the queen. West overtook and played a third round of clubs, giving East a chance to throw a heart. The effect of this was that South could not make his tenth trick by means of a heart ruff in dummy.

The play continued as follows: three rounds of trumps and then ace and king of hearts. When the nine and ten fell from East, declarer could see daylight. The position was:

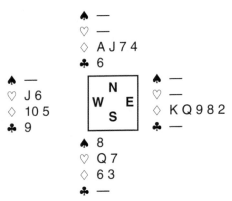

```
                ♠ —
                ♡ —
                ◇ A J 7 4
                ♣ 6
  ♠ —                        ♠ —
  ♡ J 6       ┌─────────┐    ♡ —
  ◇ 10 5      │    N    │    ◇ K Q 9 8 2
  ♣ 9         │ W     E │    ♣ —
              │    S    │
              └─────────┘
                ♠ 8
                ♡ Q 7
                ◇ 6 3
                ♣ —
```

The last spade was led and West had to discard a diamond; then a diamond was led to the ace, followed by a club on which South discarded his losing diamond; West was left on play to lead into the tenace in hearts.

An alternative throw-in

Quite often a declarer has a choice of endplays depending on the defence. The following hand was played with fine technique, but as the cards lay the defenders could have escaped the endplay:

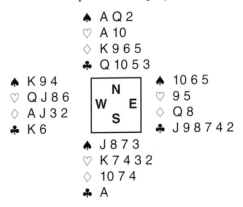

```
                ♠ A Q 2
                ♡ A 10
                ◇ K 9 6 5
                ♣ Q 10 5 3
  ♠ K 9 4                    ♠ 10 6 5
  ♡ Q J 8 6    ┌─────────┐   ♡ 9 5
  ◇ A J 3 2    │    N    │   ◇ Q 8
  ♣ K 6        │ W     E │   ♣ J 9 8 7 4 2
              │    S    │
              └─────────┘
                ♠ J 8 7 3
                ♡ K 7 4 3 2
                ◇ 10 7 4
                ♣ A
```

West opened the bidding with One Heart, North doubled, East bid Two Clubs and South Two Spades, which bought the contract. West made the unfortunate choice of the king of clubs for his opening lead.

With his slender holding South was naturally not keen on drawing trumps at once. To the second trick he led a small diamond and won with the king in dummy. The obvious play at this point seems to be to take a diamond discard on queen of clubs, but South foresaw that if he did this East would lead clubs when he got in, and there was a threat that a dangerous cross-ruff would follow. He decided, therefore, to lead a second diamond, for he thought it quite likely that East would have a doubleton honour in diamonds; in any case the queen of clubs would be good for a discard later on. So East won the next lead with the queen of diamonds and led the nine of hearts, the jack forcing the ace. Now South judged it safe to play the queen of clubs, as it was unlikely that East would be on lead again. A diamond was discarded on the club and then a diamond was ruffed. Had declarer known that East held a second heart he would have cashed the king before taking this diamond ruff, but there was a danger that East might have a singleton heart. A finesse in spades followed and then a fourth diamond, again ruffed by South. The position now was:

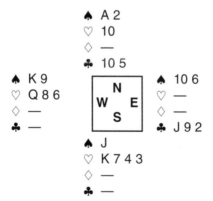

Declarer led the jack of spades, West covered with the king and dummy with ace. East saw that if he followed with a low spade another lead of spades would force him to lead into dummy's 10-5 of clubs. So East made a fine unblocking play of the ten of spades. However, declarer had an exact count of the hands, so he played a third spade, knowing that suit would break. West won and played the queen of hearts, and South let him hold this trick, so winning the last two tricks. West played too hurriedly to the eleventh trick. Had West played a low heart instead of the queen declarer would have won only one more trick.

The hand is worth careful study quite apart from the interest of the endgame. The points to note are declarer's refusal to play off the queen of clubs until the East hand was dead, and the postponement of trump leads until the count of the hand showed that East must have six clubs, two hearts, two diamonds and, therefore, three trumps.

11

Elimination Play

We saw in the last chapter that throw-in play consists of forcing an opponent to lead towards a tenace holding. Any throw-in play requires elimination, but the term 'elimination play' is generally used to describe the particular situation in which an opponent has to choose between leading towards a tenace or conceding a ruff and discard. Such a situation is shown in the following diagram:

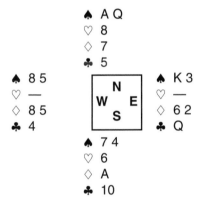

```
              ♠  A Q
              ♡  8
              ◇  7
              ♣  5
   ♠  8 5    ┌─────────┐   ♠  K 3
   ♡  —      │    N    │   ♡  —
   ◇  8 5    │  W   E  │   ◇  6 2
   ♣  4      │    S    │   ♣  Q
             └─────────┘
              ♠  7 4
              ♡  6
              ◇  A
              ♣  10
```

Hearts are trumps and declarer needs to make four of the five remaining tricks.

He first eliminates diamonds from his own hand and dummy's, then throws the lead to East with a club. East now has to make a fatal lead, either a spade to the A-Q or a diamond, conceding a ruff and discard. The coup illustrated is a 'tenace ruff and discard elimination'. The elements of the play are quite simple to recognise – a trump in both hands after all the trumps have been drawn, a tenace holding, and an opportunity to throw the lead to a player who has to make a fatal lead. When all these conditions are present, elimination play is quite easy to foresee and execute.

A simple elimination

♠ Q 6 5 3
♡ A Q 10 5 3
◇ A 6
♣ K 6

```
      N
  W       E
      S
```

♠ A K J 7 2
♡ 6 4 2
◇ 5
♣ A Q J 5

The contract is Six Spades and a diamond is led. It is quite easy for declarer to avoid the only danger - that both the heart honours are wrong. The trumps are drawn, and all cards in the minor suits played out. Then declarer leads a small heart from his own hand and finesses the ten. If East had originally K-J-x of hearts, he is left 'on play'; he must either lead back into the A-Q of hearts or lead a minor conceding a ruff and discard.

The A-Q-10 combination in the last example presented an obvious tenace situation. In many cases the tenace position is less clear. Consider the following holdings:

1	A Q 9	2	A J 10	3	K 10 5
	7 4 3		8 4 2		6 4 3

4	Q J 6	5	K 9 6	6	A 10 5
	7 5 2		J 7 3		J 9 4

These are typical combinations in which if an elimination position has been reached declarer can avoid the loss of the maximum number of tricks. For example, in diagram 1 a small card is led towards the A-Q and dummy covers whichever card West plays; if West plays low dummy plays the nine, and if West plays the ten or jack dummy plays the queen; either way declarer can be sure of losing only one trick. In diagram 3 the object is to avoid the loss of more than two tricks; a small card is led towards K-10-5 and dummy covers whichever card is played by West. Similar plays are possible with all the holdings given and with many others.

The examples given in the last paragraph were all of positions in which declarer could afford to open up the suit in which the tenace holding lay. Elimination play is equally useful in the innumerable positions in which declarer's chances are improved if the opponents can be forced to open the suit. Look at these familiar combinations:

1	A 10 7	2	K 5 3	3	K 9 6
	J 6 4		J 4 2		Q 10 5

With these holdings an extra trick is guaranteed if the opponents have to play the suit. The next three examples are of combinations which a player would prefer the opponents to open, even though an extra trick is not certain:

1	A 10 4	2	A 6	3	A 6 4
	K 9 3		Q 7		J 9 3

Of course there are countless other situations of the same type. Whenever such holdings exist, a player should be on the look-out for elimination play. Often elimination play will make a certainty of a hand which appears to depend on finesses.

Avoiding two finesses

♠ A J 9 6
♡ J 5 4
◇ A Q
♣ K 6 5 2

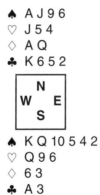

♠ K Q 10 5 4 2
♡ Q 9 6
◇ 6 3
♣ A 3

The contract is Four Spades and clubs are led. Declarer appears to have two chances: a finesse in diamonds and a finesse against the ten of hearts. Elimination play avoids the risk that both these chances may fail. Trumps are drawn, all the clubs eliminated, and the ace of diamonds played, followed by the queen. Whether the diamond finesse would have been right or wrong is immaterial; whoever has the lead now has either to concede a ruff and discard or open up hearts, assuring declarer of the one trick he needs.

Here is another hand of a rather similar type, in which elimination play provides a slight extra chance.

An extra chance

♠ A K J
♡ A 10 9 4
◇ 7 5
♣ 8 7 4 3

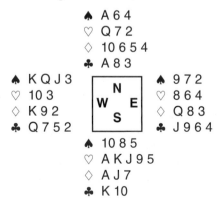

♠ 7 6 2
♡ K Q J 7 6 2
◇ K 4 3
♣ 6

The contract is Four Hearts and the defence starts off with two rounds of clubs. It looks as though declarer has to take a finesse in spades, and if this goes wrong to play East for the ace of diamonds. These chances can be slightly improved. After the trumps have been drawn and all the clubs eliminated, declarer plays ace, king and jack of spades; if West wins the trick, the contract is safe; if East wins, the contract still depends on the position of the ace of diamonds. The superiority of this line of play over taking a spade finesse is that declarer gives himself the extra chance that East may have Q-x of spades; if there were seven or eight spades in the two hands instead of only six, the chances of a doubleton queen would, of course, be much greater.

It often happens in practice that a perfect elimination cannot played, but that elimination play will still produce an extra trick if the distribution is favourable.

An imperfect elimination

♠ A 6 4
♡ Q 7 2
◇ 10 6 5 4
♣ A 8 3

♠ K Q J 3   ♠ 9 7 2
♡ 10 3   ♡ 8 6 4
◇ K 9 2   ◇ Q 8 3
♣ Q 7 5 2   ♣ J 9 6 4

♠ 10 8 5
♡ A K J 9 5
◇ A J 7
♣ K 10

As a result of moderate bidding North/South arrived at a contract of Four Hearts, although nine tricks were cold in no-trumps. West opened the king of spades and declarer in actual play went one down, losing two spades and two diamonds. Good play would have landed the contract against any defence.

As a matter of ordinary technique South should duck the first trick, and when he wins the second with the ace of spades he should consider his play carefully. There are clearly two tricks to be lost in spades, and probably two tricks in diamonds if he has to open up the suit himself. But if an opponent, and in particular West, can be made to lead the suit, then only one diamond need be lost. The difficulty appears to lie in the fact that South cannot draw all the trumps and still have one trump left in each hand. But suppose West has only two trumps? If this is so, elimination will succeed. South lays down the ace and king of hearts, eliminates the clubs, and leads a spade. Now, as the cards lie, West can make no lead which does not concede a trick. Note that it is essential to the success of his play that the declarer should play the two top trumps from his own hand, retaining the queen in dummy; if he does not do this West can lead his last spade and East will overruff the dummy.

There are some situations in which the advantages of elimination play are not at all easy to recognise.

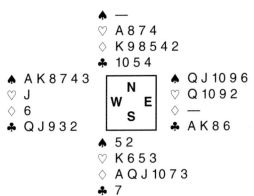

East/West bid to Six Spades and North/South sacrificed in Seven Diamonds. This contract appears to go three down, the defence making a club and two hearts. The correct play is neat; if hearts are not attacked by the defence, the black suits are eliminated, then a low heart is led, ducked in both hands. This play is foolproof against any 4-1 distribution, unless the singleton is the two; for if the singleton wins, the player must concede a ruff and discard, and if East overtakes he cannot play back a heart without setting up a finesse position.

There is one frequent combination in which the advantage of elimination play is particularly useful. It arises when the hands of declarer and dummy hold the ace of a suit and the jack unsupported. This hand is an example:

A-J elimination

```
        ♠ 6 5
        ♡ K 6
        ◇ J 7 5 3 2
        ♣ K J 4 2
            N
        W       E
            S
        ♠ 4
        ♡ A Q 5
        ◇ A 8 6
        ♣ A Q 7 6 5 3
```

In Five Clubs declarer seems to be in danger of losing a spade and two diamonds. The best play, after a spade lead, is as follows: draw the trumps, lead a low diamond from dummy towards the ace, and then eliminate the major suits. After this there is a good chance that when you play a second round of diamonds the defence will be unable to cash their two winners and that the player who wins the next trick will have to concede a ruff and discard. This play is certain to succeed, for example, if East had originally K-4 or Q-4. The defenders can, if they are wide awake, defend the hand if the original distribution of diamonds is:

```
                    J 7 5 3 2
      Q 9 (or K 9)              K 10 4 (or Q 10 4)
                    A 8 6
```

When the ace is played West should foresee the endplay and unblock by dropping his high card. To make this play more difficult for West, declarer should play the ace of diamonds as early as possible in the hand - before he has eliminated spades and hearts.

Two lines of play

The value of elimination play is not apparent at first sight in the hand which follows; there are as a matter of fact two ways of playing the hand, both leading to elimination positions.

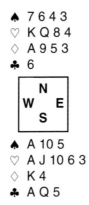

♠ 7 6 4 3
♡ K Q 8 4
◇ A 9 5 3
♣ 6

♠ A 10 5
♡ A J 10 6 3
◇ K 4
♣ A Q 5

South reached a rather ambitious contract of Six Hearts after West made an intervening call of One Spade. The jack of clubs was led and East's king fell to the ace. The trumps were drawn in two rounds. It looked as though there were two losers in spades, but remembering that West had overcalled with One Spade declarer saw the possibility of an elimination. As West had not led a spade, it was unlikely that he held K-Q-J; there was, therefore, a good chance that East held a singleton honour, probably the queen. So declarer played the queen of clubs, discarding a diamond from dummy, took three rounds of diamonds, ruffed the last club, and then played a low spade from both hands. The situation at this point was:

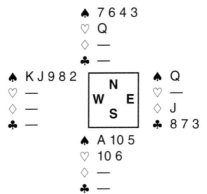

♠ 7 6 4 3
♡ Q
◇ —
♣ —

♠ K J 9 8 2
♡ —
◇ —
♣ —

♠ Q
♡ —
◇ J
♣ 8 7 3

♠ A 10 5
♡ 10 6
◇ —
♣ —

Whether East or West wins the spade trick, the elimination play succeeds.

The hand is interesting because the contract might have been made in another way. If East has a singleton spade and at least four diamonds, loser on loser play is successful. On the queen of clubs declarer discards a spade from dummy; he then takes three rounds of diamonds, cashes the ace of spades, ruffs out the last club and plays the fourth diamond from dummy, throwing a spade from his own hand and letting East hold the trick. East, if he has not a second spade, must now concede a ruff and discard.

Loser on loser eliminations are among the most attractive plays in the game. The next hand is a standard example.

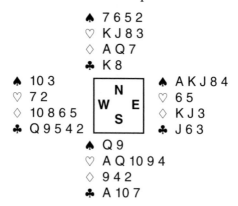

South plays in Four Hearts after East has made an opening bid of One Spade. Spades are led and declarer trumps the third round.

If declarer follows the ordinary routine of eliminating all the spades and clubs and leading a low diamond at the tenth trick, he makes the hand if West carelessly plays low; for then the seven can be put on from dummy and East is left on play. This line of play is defeated if West correctly plays the eight so that the lead cannot be ducked into East's hand.

Loser on loser play makes the hand against any defence. South draws trumps, ruffs out the clubs and then plays the last spade from dummy, discarding a diamond from his own hand. East has then either to lead up to the diamonds or concede a ruff and discard.

Some very complicated positions can arise after a loser on loser elimination. Declarer may not have foreseen the effect of his play on the next hand, but good technique led him to play correctly.

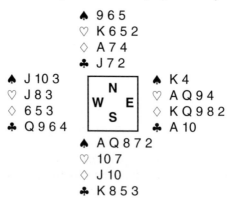

The contract was a simple Two Spades, after East had bid both diamonds and hearts. West led a diamond and East held the first trick. East led the ace of clubs to the second trick and followed with another club which South won.

Declarer saw little advantage in entering dummy to take the spade finesse, so he laid down the ace, then entered dummy with the ace of diamonds and played a trump; East won with the king and played a diamond, on which South, instead of ruffing, discarded a heart; the position at this point was:

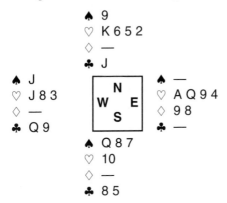

After holding the trick in diamonds East was faced with a choice of plays, all of which are to declarer's advantage. In practice East made what looks like the best lead of another diamond; declarer discarded a heart from his own hand, West ruffed and made only one more trick. East might have played the ace of hearts before leading the diamond. If he does, South discards a club from both hands and West makes only a trump trick. Finally, East can play ace and another heart; then South draws the trump and concedes only one club.

The result of the hand is that by this play South goes one down in Two Spades instead of two down. It is rather puzzling to see how declarer gains an extra trick after giving up a diamond which he does not have to lose, and after allowing West to make the jack of spades. The explanation is that the diamond trick is immediately recovered through the discard of the heart loser; and when the defence makes the jack of spades declarer discards a loser and gains the extra trick because dummy's last trump becomes available for ruffing.

Defence to elimination play

The principal defence to elimination play lies in the simple unblock so that the wrong player is not left in the lead. A defender must take care not to be caught napping in the position which arose on the following hand:

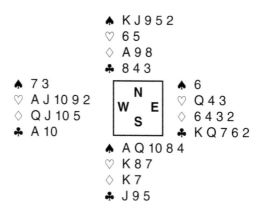

South became declarer in Three Spades after East/West had bid up to Three Hearts. A diamond was led and after drawing trumps South eliminated diamonds, entered dummy with a trump, and led a club. East knew that his side needed three tricks from clubs, so he did not split his honours; declarer played the nine and West won with the ten; after cashing the ace of clubs West had to lead a heart or concede a ruff and discard. Of course, West should have won the club lead with the ace; his partner had already discarded a low heart and the only hope was that East held K-Q of clubs and the queen of hearts.

A pseudo elimination

A declarer has many chances to create the appearance of an elimination position when in fact there is one suit which the defenders can lead without loss. Sometimes the defenders can be put to a difficult guess.

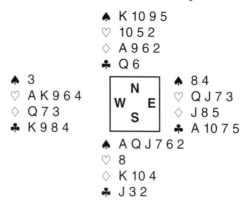

West led two rounds of hearts against a contract of Four Spades. Declarer drew trumps and ruffed the last heart. There was little hope of avoiding a diamond loser unless the opponents could be persuaded to lead the suit.

This they might do if they thought that a third round of clubs would allow a ruff and discard. So, to create the impression that he had a doubleton club, South led the jack from his own hand. West won with the king and played a club back. It seemed to East most improbable that South had three clubs to the jack, the more so as East held the ten himself; so, on play after winning with the ace of clubs, East led a diamond and the defence lost its trick in this suit.

Declarer's play of the jack of clubs was psychologically a clever stroke. Nevertheless, there was a line of reasoning which should have guided East to make the right defence; if South had a doubleton club, then his distribution must be 6-4-2-1 and if South had four diamonds, then a ruff and discard would not help him, so a club could be led without danger. As so often, careful counting was the clue to the right defence.

12

Trump Coups

There are several forms of endplay whose character depends on the element of trumps. A simple trump coup occurs when an opponent's minor tenace in trumps is picked up by means of plain suit leads from dummy:

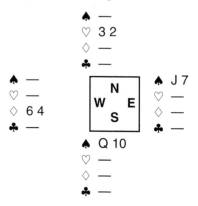

Spades are trumps and if the lead is in dummy East makes no more tricks.

To bring this situation about it is always necessary for declarer to reduce the length of his own trump suit to that of the opponent on his right. Trump coups are usually easy to execute, but to prepare for them often needs foresight.

Trump reducing play

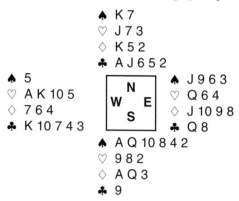

The contract is Four Spades and the defenders lead off with three rounds of hearts, followed by a diamond which declarer wins. The only danger lies in a possible trump loser. If South draws two rounds of trumps straight away he will find that he cannot bring off the endplay against East. It is true that South can shorten his hand twice by ruffing clubs, but there will be no third entry to dummy for the vital lead at the twelfth trick. Declarer should, as a matter of technique, take one ruff in clubs before touching trumps. Then ace and another spade are led; if West follows there is nothing to worry about. If West shows out on the second lead of spades, then a second club is ruffed. By this time declarer's trumps are reduced to the same length as East's and there is still the king of diamonds as an entry to dummy for the lead of a plain suit at trick twelve.

A grand coup

When the cards which declarer ruffs in order to shorten his hand are winning cards, the play is described as a grand coup. This play was at one time considered the summit of brilliance, but it is recognised nowadays that it is neither rare nor difficult. In the following hand a grand coup is combined with a throw-in in trumps.

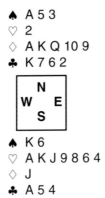

        ♠ A 5 3
        ♡ 2
        ◇ A K Q 10 9
        ♣ K 7 6 2

        ♠ K 6
        ♡ A K J 9 8 6 4
        ◇ J
        ♣ A 5 4

Against Six Hearts a club was led and won in dummy. The jack of hearts was finessed at the second trick and West showed out. This meant that East had Q-10-7-5-3 and the contract could be made only by means of an endplay in trumps, for which it was necessary to prepare by reducing declarer's trumps to the same number as East's. The jack of diamonds was led and overtaken and a club was discarded on a second diamond, then a third diamond was ruffed; this was a grand coup, for the card that was ruffed was a winner. The ace of clubs was cashed, followed by the king and ace of spades. A double grand coup was then achieved by the lead of another diamond, ruffed by declarer. This left South with A-K-9-8 against East's Q-10-7-5, and the lead of a low trump left East on play.

An under-trumping grand coup

Occasionally declarer effects the reduction of his own trumps by means of an underruff. Opportunities for this play are not so infrequent. This is a hand from match play:

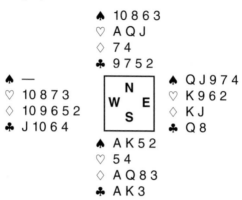

The contract was Four Spades, doubled by East. A low club was opened and the queen fell to the ace. A heart finesse lost to the king and East led a club. Declarer won, took a club discard on the hearts, and finessed the queen of diamonds. Still avoiding any lead of trumps, he played ace and another diamond, ruffing with dummy's 8. East overruffed and made his best return, the queen of spades. South won and ruffed the fourth diamond with the ten, East again overruffing. The position was:

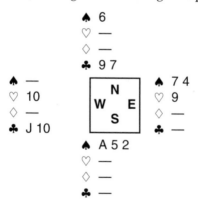

East returned the heart; this was his best play, for it gave declarer a chance to go wrong. However, South was not to be caught napping at this stage; he took care to overruff in dummy, and East's last two trumps were picked up by the A-5. Despite his fine original holding in trumps, East made only two of them,

A quadruple trump-reducing play

Sometimes declarer has to reduce his trumps three and even four times in order to bring about the required position. The following hand was the subject of much analysis when it was played in a pairs competition.

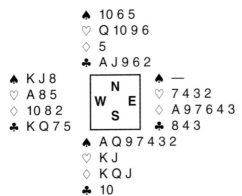

West dealt and bid One Club; the final contract was Four Spades by South, doubled by West. The opening lead was the ten of diamonds and a heart was the usual return. At one table declarer made his contract by the following play: he used dummy's entries to ruff three clubs and one heart in his own hand, and so reduced his trumps to A-Q-9; then he brought off an endplay against West. It was generally held at the time that West could have defeated this play by holding up the ace of hearts at trick two. In fact this is not so. Declarer plays the ace of clubs, ruffs a club, and wins the next four tricks with two diamond ruffs in dummy and two club ruffs in his own hand; he then plays the jack of hearts and West is forced to present him with another ruff. There is only one return which East can make to beat the contract, and that is very difficult to foresee. If East leads a diamond at the second trick, South has to use this entry to dummy before the ace of clubs has been played and so before he is ready to make use of the entry; after this he cannot obtain the four ruffs needed in his own hand.

The coup en passant

A trump coup combined with a loser on loser play provides what is known as the coup en passant, this term being based on the pawn capture en passant at chess.

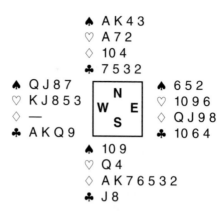

The contract is Three Diamonds and West leads three rounds of clubs. South plays the ace of diamonds and finds that he has two certain losers in trumps. This looks like one down, but the contract can made by accurate play. A spade is led to the ace and a fourth club is ruffed; then the king of spades, followed by another spade, which is ruffed. This leaves:

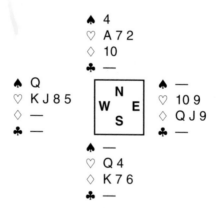

Declarer plays off the top diamond, enters dummy with the ace of hearts, and plays the last spade; if East trumps, South discards the losing heart, and if East discards, South makes an extra trick in trumps.

West's club lead at trick three was a tactical error. Instead of helping declarer to shorten his trumps, West should switch to the queen of spades.

Avoiding a guess in trumps

We noticed in the last chapter that the various forms of endplay are often mixed with one another. The next hand combines the technique of elimination play with the trump-reducing play which is the sign of a trump coup:

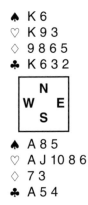

```
          ♠ K 6
          ♡ K 9 3
          ◇ 9 8 6 5
          ♣ K 6 3 2
              N
          W       E
              S
          ♠ A 8 5
          ♡ A J 10 8 6
          ◇ 7 3
          ♣ A 5 4
```

The contract is Four Hearts and West leads a low diamond. Three rounds of diamonds are played, South ruffing the third round. A club has to be lost, so the contract depends upon not losing to the queen of trumps.

The play is quite simple; the ace and king of clubs are played, followed by king, ace and another spade ruffed; dummy's last diamond is led and if East discards, declarer can ruff without danger. By this time he has reduced his trumps to three and he exits with a club, forcing the opponents to play hearts.

Avoiding a trump loser

The technique on the following hand is more advanced.

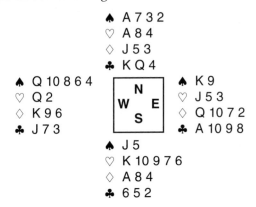

```
                    ♠ A 7 3 2
                    ♡ A 8 4
                    ◇ J 5 3
                    ♣ K Q 4
♠ Q 10 8 6 4                         ♠ K 9
♡ Q 2              N                 ♡ J 5 3
◇ K 9 6       W        E             ◇ Q 10 7 2
♣ J 7 3           S                 ♣ A 10 9 8
                    ♠ J 5
                    ♡ K 10 9 7 6
                    ◇ A 8 4
                    ♣ 6 5 2
```

The contract was Two Hearts. West led the six of spades, dummy played low, East won and returned a spade. Declarer could see that outside the trump suit there was a losing spade and two losing diamonds and possibly two losing clubs. If he was going to avoid losing a trick in hearts he would have to reduce his trumps, so at the third trick he led a spade and ruffed. A club followed, East won with the ace and played a club back.

Then the fourth spade was ruffed, the ace of diamonds was cashed, and the lead surrendered. The defenders made their three winners in the minor suits and then had to broach trumps; declarer played for split honours and so avoided the loss of any trump trick.

A trump pick-up

This chapter concludes with four examples of hands in which the opponents' trump tricks disappear quite mysteriously. Study this diagram:

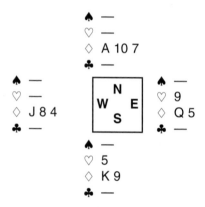

Diamonds are trumps and South has the lead. East and West have an apparently certain trick between them, but when the five of hearts is led the defenders' trump trick disappears. Opportunities for this play are not common because to make it possible the distribution of the opposing hands has to follow an exact pattern.

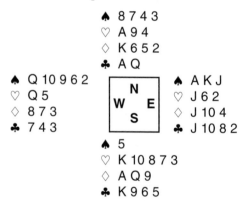

South plays in Six Hearts, and spades are led and continued. It would not be unreasonable for declarer to decide that his best chance was to drop the Q-J of trumps; but as the cards lie, the contract can be made although the trump honours are split. Declarer ruffs two spades makes three top diamonds and three top clubs. This leaves:

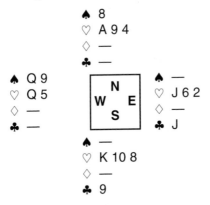

South leads the club, West discards and dummy ruffs; then a spade is led from dummy and the defenders are helpless.

The lead of a plain card when the opponent who is last to play has to follow can produce quite freakish effects. The next hand was played in only Three Diamonds and declarer probably did not foresee the ending; nevertheless, the play is instructive.

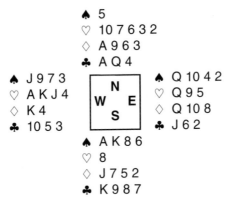

The king of hearts was led, followed by another heart, which declarer ruffed. It looks impossible to make eleven tricks in diamonds, for apparently there are two certain losers in trumps. However, the play continued as follows: four rounds of spades, a heart ruff and three rounds of clubs. The position was:

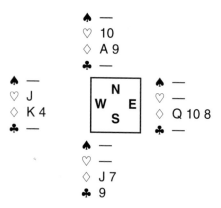

The last heart was led from dummy and East ruffed with the queen - the only play to give the defence a chance of making two tricks. To the twelfth trick East led the eight of diamonds, but declarer read the position correctly and played low, so that the defenders were held to one trick in hearts and one in trumps.

Smother play

Another end position in which the defenders' trump trick disappears quite unexpectedly is the following:

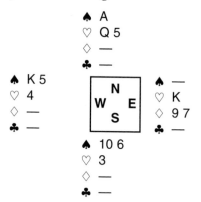

Spades are trumps, and West may well think he is going to make a trump trick. But South leads a heart, won by East, and East has to return a diamond. Declarer plays a trump, and dummy overruffs or not, according to the card played by West. This is called a smother play, and it bears a resemblance to a smothered mate at chess. It is a coup seldom brought off in actual play because, as with the trump pick-up, it is possible only when the opposing cards follow an exact pattern.

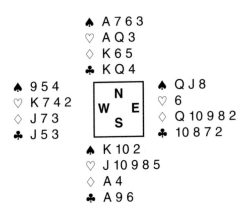

West leads a spade against Six Hearts. When East shows out on the second round of trumps there is only one hope. Declarer takes three rounds of diamonds and three rounds of clubs and cashes the ace of spades, leaving this position:

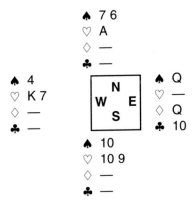

A spade is led and the defenders make only one trick.

The vanishing trick

A combination of trump coup and throw-in play produces a curious result in this ending:

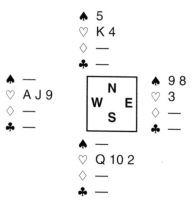

Hearts are trumps and a spade is led from dummy; declarer ruffs with the queen and West is held to one trump trick. The following hand shows one of the few examples recorded of this coup in actual play:

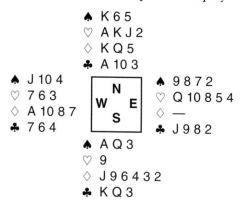

West led the jack of spades against Six Diamonds, and declarer won in his own hand and led a low trump. The queen won but East showed out. It looked as though West, with A-10-8 over J-9-6, was bound to make two tricks, but declarer saw one chance and played for it. He ruffed two hearts in hand, as it was necessary to shorten his trumps, and played out three rounds of both black suits. Luckily for declarer, West had follow suit all the time. The lead was left in dummy at trick eleven, and the position was:

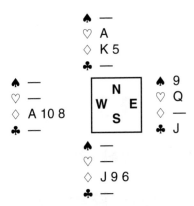

The ace of hearts was led and ruffed by declarer's jack. West's second trump trick vanished into thin air.

13

Squeeze Play –
The Basic Principles

Squeeze play, in which an opponent is forced to throw away winning cards (or cards which protect winners), is the most rewarding form of endplay and has the reputation of being the most difficult. It is true that very complex problems can be built around it, and it is also true that squeeze play has to be learned - it cannot be picked up; but for all that, once the general idea is grasped, it is a good deal easier to become adept at squeeze play than to be good in the defence to a tricky contract of Two Diamonds.

Perhaps it is necessary to explain that squeeze play consists of more than leading out a long suit and hoping that the opponents will throw a wrong card. That is what is called a pseudo-squeeze. Against a genuine squeeze the opponents are helpless. They are forced to discard winners and so allow declarer to make tricks which at first sight may seem impossible.

The root of the matter is this: two hands, say those of declarer and dummy, may contain between them more vital cards than one opponent can protect; so that when one opponent needs to keep winners or guards in more than one suit, pressure of space may compel him to relinquish his hold on one suit or the other. Study this diagram, which shows a squeeze in its simplest and also its commonest form:

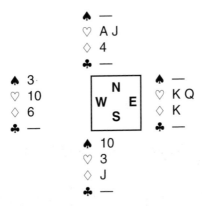

In this three-card ending East has to protect both hearts and diamonds; when South leads the ten of spades, discarding a diamond from dummy, East has the same threats to meet and cannot cope. Now in this simple position certain basic elements are present which are common to every squeeze situation. Follow carefully as we analyse them; they must be understood before you can make any progress.

1. Menaces

The two cards that bother East are the jack of hearts and the jack of diamonds. These cards threaten East and are called 'menaces'. In any squeeze situation there must be at least two menaces, and if there are only two they must lie against the same opponent: that is the opponent's dilemma: and a dilemma must have two horns. Furthermore (because of the need to go from hand to hand) at least one of these two menaces must be accompanied by a winning card; in the present example the A-J of hearts represents such a menace, called a two-card menace.

2. Entries

It is understood, then, that in the position we are studying, the jack of diamonds is a one-card menace, the A-J of hearts a two-card menace. The three of hearts in South's hand is vital as an entry card to the two-card menace. There must be such an entry card: a weapon is no good if you cannot reach it.

3. Squeeze card

The ten of spades is the squeeze card - the one that turns the screw. There is this to remember about the squeeze card: it must be in the hand opposite to the two-card menace.

4. Timing

You will notice that in the diagram there were three tricks to go and South could win two by top cards; to put it another way declarer was in the position of being able to win all the tricks but one. This is not an invariable condition of squeeze play, but what can be laid down is this: at the moment when the squeeze begins there must not be any superfluous card which the opponent who is to be squeezed can let go without damaging his hand. The importance of this may be difficult to understand at this point; but this much you can see, that if in the diagram situation a small club is added to each hand, West holding the master club, no squeeze is on. The position must be 'tight'.

There is a further point to be noticed in connection with the position of the menace cards. In the diagram overleaf, the one-card menace, the jack of diamonds, was in the same hand as the squeeze card and opposite the two-card menace. The two menaces can be put in the same hand, but then they are effective only if the opponent who is to be squeezed plays in front of them.

Now the menaces are in the same hand and the squeeze still works; but if the East and West hands are transposed the squeeze fails, for North has to discard before the opponent to be squeezed. The discussion up to this point is bound to seem somewhat arid and removed from the game. However, as was remarked earlier, squeeze play has to be studied in a way different from any other branch of play. You should, by now, have a grasp of the essentials: the two menaces, one of them a two-card menace, threatening the same opponent; the squeeze card in the hand opposite to the two-card menace; and the time element, whose effect is usually that the squeeze begins when the player has the means to win all the remaining tricks but one.

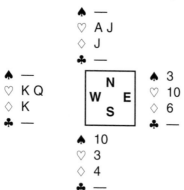

The next step is to study some exercises in squeeze play. You will find that in every instance the arrangement of menaces and entry cards conforms to the rules given above.

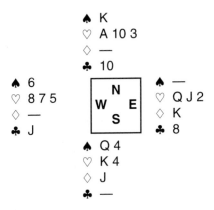

No-trumps; South to lead

First of all make a note of the number of cards left and of the number of tricks which declarer can win by top cards. In this example there are five cards left and South can win four tricks by top cards. As there are no tenace positions, the fifth can come only from a squeeze. To bring off the squeeze, South must find two menace cards threatening the same opponent. These are not difficult to find in the diagram. There are no menaces in spades, for there are no losers; in hearts there is a two-card menace against East; in diamonds the jack is a menace against East and in clubs the ten menaces West.

Well, we have found what we want - two menaces against one player, East. The next step is to reduce the situation in our minds to a three-card ending. This you should be able to do. The order of play is to lead a spade towards the king, come back to the king of hearts, and play the squeeze card, the queen of spades.

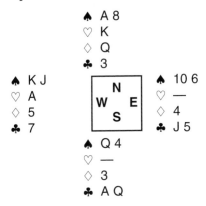

No-trumps; South to lead

Once more South can make four of the five remaining tricks by top cards. The next step, remember, is to look for the menaces. It may help to draw a pencilled circle round a card which you see is a menace with an arrow pointing towards the player whom it threatens. In the diagram there is a menace against West in hearts, and also in spades. The spade position represents what is called a 'two-card split menace'. It serves the purpose of an ordinary two-card menace so long as the one-card menace (the king of hearts) is in the same hand as the controlling card (the ace of spades), as it is here, and both menaces are 'over' the opponent who is to be squeezed.

The order of play is to lead a diamond to the queen and then play the two top clubs, squeezing West. Note that if you play the clubs at the beginning the squeeze does not work. What happens in effect is that dummy is squeezed before West; the reason in theory why things have gone wrong is that the squeeze card, in this order of play the queen of diamonds, is in the same hand as the two-card menace. You see how knowledge of theory stops you from playing the cards in the wrong order; you have to play the diamond first, so that the squeeze comes from South.

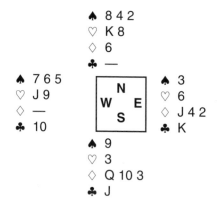

No-trumps; South to lead

There are six cards left, and with the help of the finesse in diamonds South can make five tricks by top cards. Let us look at the menaces. Dummy's last spade is a menace against West; in hearts there is a two-card menace against West. Against East there is a one-card menace in clubs and a two-card menace in diamonds. So it appears at first sight that either opponent can be squeezed.

Theoretically there is no reason why this should not be so, and indeed it often happens that way. But as the cards lie in this example, there is a practical reason why the squeeze against West fails. Can you see what it is? Well, what happens if you try to squeeze West? To make your two tricks in diamonds you have to enter dummy with the king of hearts for the finesse. When you have done that you have no two-card menace against West and so cannot squeeze him. The squeeze against East succeeds. The nine of spades is played off, dummy is entered with the king of hearts, and the eight of spades squeezes East in the minor suits.

In the next example, again, it may seem at first sight that either opponent can be squeezed:

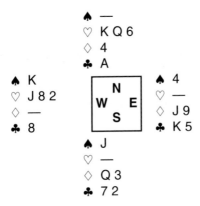

No-trumps; South to lead

There are menaces against West in the major suits, against East in the minors. But in practice you can do nothing against West because there is no entry to the two-card menace. So a club is led and East is squeezed on the second round of hearts.

If the terminology used in this chapter about 'menaces' and squeeze cards' is new to you, you are bound to wonder whether a declarer in actual play works out a hand in these terms.

Probably not, in so many words. But a declarer who understands what is wanted knows what to look for. Experience enables him to reduce a hand in his mind to a three-card ending which is the matrix of a squeeze. The value of studying miniature exercises in squeeze play is that it accustoms the player to visualise the end position which he has to bring about. After a while it becomes quite easy to glance at a diagram of all 52 cards and say at once that an opponent can be squeezed in certain suits.

14

Examples of the Simple Squeeze

The term 'simple squeeze' has a special meaning: it refers to the type of squeeze described in the last chapter, in which one opponent is squeezed in two suits. In the following examples, therefore, the declarer has to look for menace cards in two suits lying exclusively against one opponent.

Squeeze card in dummy

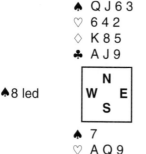

```
            ♠ Q J 6 3
            ♡ 6 4 2
            ◇ K 8 5
            ♣ A J 9

                  N
♠8 led        W       E
                  S

            ♠ 7
            ♡ A Q 9
            ◇ A Q 4
            ♣ K Q 8 7 5 3
```

North/South reach a contract of Six Clubs after East had opened the bidding with One Spade. The eight of spades is led, dummy covers with the jack, and East wins with the king. At trick two East leads the jack of hearts and declarer finesses the queen, which holds the trick.

South is one trick short of his contract and the extra trick can come only from a squeeze. Menaces exist in spades and hearts, and it is reasonable to assume that the control of both suits lies with East. It looks as though the queen of spades is a menace against the ace, and the A-9 of hearts a two-card menace against the K-10.

So the ingredients are there; all that remains is not to spoil them in the cooking. This can happen only if declarer overlooks that since the two-card menace is in his own hand, the squeeze card must come from the hand opposite, the dummy. All the clubs must be played off, and then three rounds of diamonds, finishing in dummy. This is the end position:

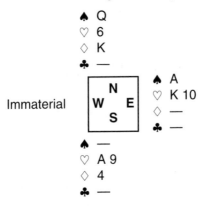

The king of diamonds is the squeeze card.

Isolating the menace

It is necessary sometimes to take special steps to establish a menace card against a single opponent.

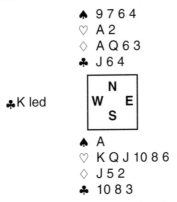

The contract is Four Hearts. The defenders win three tricks in clubs and then East leads a heart.

South has to assume that the diamond finesse is right. If West has K-x of diamonds declarer is home, but if the king is twice guarded an extra trick has to be found from somewhere.

If West has K-x-x of diamonds, which as declarer you should assume, you have a split two-card menace against him. Can you find another menace against West? Spades are the only hope, and at first sight they may seem a poor hope, because no doubt East has a card to beat dummy's nine, and so long as East can look after the spades, West is in no difficulty. However, there is this chance – that West started with five spades and East with only three. If this is so, by ruffing out two rounds of spades you can leave West with sole control of the suit, which is what you want.

You have to be careful about entries. You remember that a heart was returned at trick four; win in your own hand, play off the ace of spades, enter dummy with the ace of hearts, and ruff a spade. When you have drawn the trumps, finesse the queen of diamonds and ruff a spade. Then play out all the trumps and hope for a little luck. If West had originally five spades and three or more diamonds to the king, your play is rewarded.

The play of ruffing out two rounds of spades, in the hope of leaving West in sole control of the suit, is known as 'isolating the menace'. It is very common, and a good player does it quite automatically on many hands, sometimes with effect, sometimes not.

Vienna coup

The next hand shows another stratagem used in preparation for a squeeze. In order that a one-card menace may be correctly positioned for a squeeze against the right-hand opponent, a master card in the opposite hand is played off before the squeeze begins. The play is known as the Vienna coup.

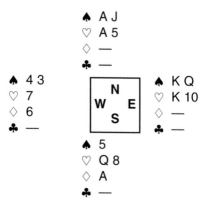

East has to guard two suits and it looks as though a squeeze is on; but when the ace of diamonds is played, North has to discard before East, and this spoils the position. Now imagine that the ace of hearts has been played off earlier in the hand; then if East lets go a heart on the ace of diamonds South can make the queen and all is well. The Vienna coup is really an unblocking play; to bring off the coup in actual play requires good understanding of squeeze positions.

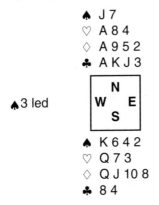

South plays Three No-Trumps and West leads the three of spades. The jack is put up from dummy, East covers with the queen, and South wins with the king. The diamond finesse loses and three rounds of spades are won by the defence, dummy discarding a heart and a diamond. A diamond follows, won in dummy; the position is:

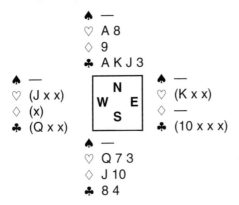

The lead is in dummy and declarer needs all the remaining tricks. He has only one hope: that the club finesse is right and that the long clubs and the king of hearts are held by the same player. As it may be East who holds these cards, the ace of hearts must be played off before declarer returns to hand; otherwise dummy, holding both the menaces, will have to discard in front of the player who is to be squeezed. The Vienna coup has the effect of transferring to South the menace in hearts.

Transferring the menace

The Vienna coup is a way of transferring a menace from one attacking hand to the other. A variation of the coup accomplishes a different object: it transfers control of a menace from one defending hand to the other.

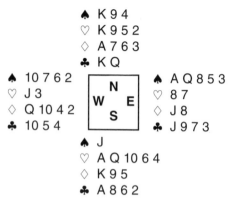

West led a low spade against a contract of Six Hearts. The queen of spades won the first trick and East returned a club. The trumps fell in two rounds, but declarer had still to dispose of the apparent loser in diamonds. The first thought that occurred to South was that a squeeze would be on if East had four diamonds in addition to the ace of spades but when East followed to two rounds of trumps and four rounds of clubs, it seemed improbable that he would have four diamonds as well; in fact, it was more likely that West had the long diamonds. The position was:

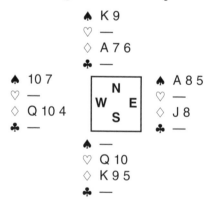

South could not be sure who held the ten of spades, but hoping it was West he led the king from dummy. This had the effect of transferring control of the suit from East to West, so that when the last heart was played West was squeezed in spades and diamonds.

The criss-cross squeeze

We shall find in the next chapter that many variations in the arrangement of menaces and entries are possible so long as some sort of compensation exists. In this end position:

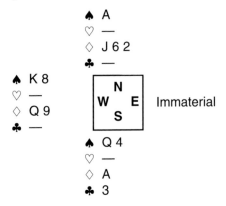

the three of clubs squeezes West, although there is no two-card menace of the kind usually found. Compensation exists in the form of the two quick entries. This is known as a criss-cross squeeze; the lie of the heart suit in the following hand is a typical symptom.

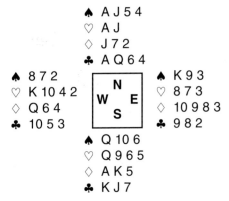

A spade was led against Six No-Trumps; East won with the king and returned a diamond, won by South. The heart finesse followed, making eleven tricks on top. Had there been a small heart in dummy as well as the A-J there would have been a straightforward squeeze against West; as it was, declarer had to use the criss-cross method. After six tricks had been won in the black suits the position was:

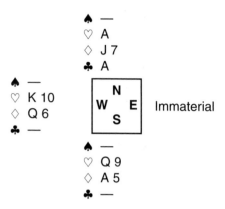

The ace of clubs was led from dummy and a diamond discarded from hand, forcing West to unguard one of the red suits. Note that if the ace of hearts had been played off earlier in the hand the contract could not have been made.

Losing a trick after the squeeze

In the examples of squeeze play given up to now, declarer has been in the position of being able to win all the remaining tricks but one; after the squeeze card has been played no tricks have been lost. It is not always so; a defender who has controlling cards in two suits sometimes wins a trick after the squeeze has begun. Study this diagram:

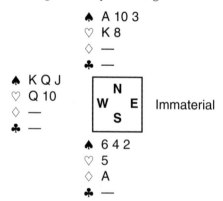

There are five cards left and South has only three tricks on top when he plays the squeeze card, the ace of diamonds. However, West cannot stand the pressure and although he wins one more trick he has to concede to dummy an extra spade or heart. Note that if the ace of spades had been played off, the squeeze would still have been effective. The ending would have been similar to that which arose on the following hand:

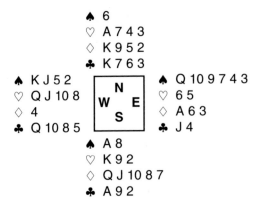

West led the queen of hearts against Five Diamonds, and when East won with the ace of trumps he led another heart, forcing out the second control. South ruffed a spade and drew trumps, leading to this position:

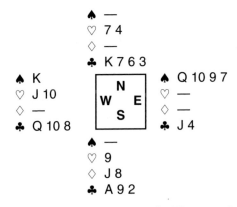

South could afford to lose one more trick. The usual way to tackle a situation of this kind is to lose that trick as soon as possible and so rectify the count for a squeeze. As the cards lie, this cannot be done; if declarer plays a heart, West will win and play a fourth round, killing the menace; and if a club is ducked West will win and play off the good heart. The contract can be made only by playing off the two diamonds. West can discard a spade on the first but is squeezed on the second. This is not an easy type of endplay to foresee or to plan. As a rule declarer can reduce the position to the familiar pattern in which he has a two-card menace and a one-card menace against the same opponent. For example, in the present hand, if it had not been for the danger of a ruff declarer could have ducked one round of hearts early on; that would have made the timing right for the usual form of ending. The stratagem of ducking a trick in order to make the timing right for a squeeze is discussed in the next section.

Rectifying the count

The last hand showed that there are exceptions to the general rule that a squeeze is effective only when declarer can win all the remaining tricks but one. The squeeze was effective because all West's cards were 'busy'. If a defender has a superfluous card which he can discard without loss when the squeeze card is played, then the squeeze peters out. Study this diagram:

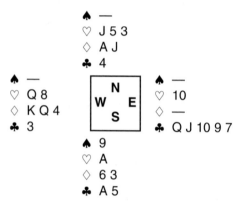

South wants five of the last six tricks and East, who has the lead, plays the queen of clubs. If declarer takes this trick he is defeated, for when the nine of spades is played West can discard a diamond without damaging his hand. Declarer can afford to lose one trick, and he should lose it as early as possible and in such a way that the entries essential for the squeeze are not affected. The right play is to duck to the queen of clubs. On a second club West can discard a diamond, but when the squeeze card is played West is helpless. The process of dropping a trick in order to make the timing right for a squeeze is known as 'rectifying the count'. Here is a simple example:

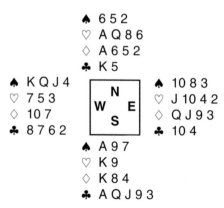

West leads the king of spades against Six No-Trumps. South can count eleven tricks on top, and since his only hope of a twelfth lies in a successful squeeze he allows West to hold the first trick. West probably continues spades, South wins and plays off five rounds of clubs, discarding a spade and two diamonds from dummy. On the last club East is squeezed in the red suits.

If South had won the opening lead he would have had no play for the contract. On the last club he would have had to discard a diamond from dummy and East would also have discarded a diamond. Declarer would be left with a loser in each red suit and would have no way of bringing pressure to bear on East.

The submarine squeeze

The last hand was a fairly simple one to play because the opportunity to lose a trick at the right moment was directly presented by the opening lead. When declarer does the work himself, playing a low card from both hands when he holds the master, the play is known as the 'submarine squeeze'. It is a common manoeuvre, and in the following hand is combined with reverse dummy play.

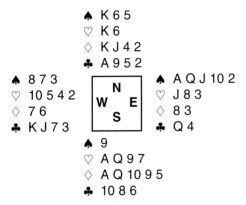

The contract was Five Diamonds and the opening lead was won by East with the ten of spades. The best return would have been a heart, but the squeeze was not easy to foresee and in practice East led a trump to the second trick. South won, and having ten tricks on top ducked a round of clubs so that the count would be right for a possible squeeze. East returned another trump and South ruffed two spades in his own hand so that dummy had the long trump. The end position was:

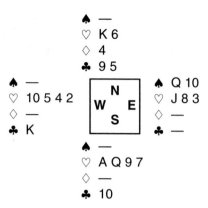

The lead was in dummy and the last trump proved too much for West. This was a well-played hand, for the combination of reverse dummy and squeeze was easy to miss. A weaker player would have ruffed a heart in dummy, not realising that in effect he was ruffing a valuable menace card in the long trump hand.

Loser on loser again

It happens quite often that declarer wants to lose a trick to rectify the count but can see no way of doing so without surrendering one of the menaces which he needs for the squeeze. The familiar loser-on-loser play is sometimes the way out of this difficulty.

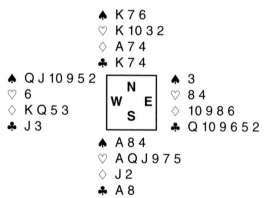

South becomes declarer in Six Hearts after West had made an overcall of One Spade. The queen of spades was led and won in the closed hand. Prospects seemed moderate, for although it was quite likely that West had the king and queen of diamonds in addition to spade control, the timing was wrong for a squeeze. A trick cannot be given up in spades or diamonds without sacrificing the menace card in the suit played. The solution is rather unexpected. After drawing trumps South plays three rounds of clubs, and instead of ruffing the third round he discards a losing spade. East leads a diamond, won by the ace, and then declarer runs the trump suit. At the eleventh trick West is squeezed in spades and diamonds.

15

Advanced Squeeze Play

A squeeze which involves both opponents is known as a double squeeze. The simplest form of double squeeze is shown in this diagram:

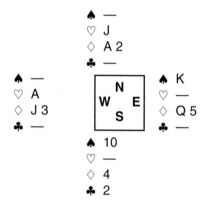

South leads the two of clubs and as he must hold on to the ace of hearts West throws a diamond. Dummy discards the jack of hearts and East is squeezed. You will notice that the ingredients of this squeeze are two one-card menaces, the jack of hearts and ten of spades, and a two-card menace in diamonds which both opponents control. The diamond holding is known as a 'double menace'. These are the usual ingredients for a double squeeze: one suit which both opponents control and two suits which they control separately. The position overleaf reduces to a three-card ending because both the one-card menaces are favourably situated on the left of the players whom they threaten. When the menaces are so placed, the double squeeze is quite easy to play.

Double squeeze and Vienna coup

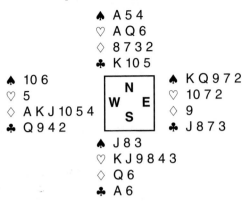

```
            ♠ A 5 4
            ♡ A Q 6
            ◇ 8 7 3 2
            ♣ K 10 5
♠ 10 6                        ♠ K Q 9 7 2
♡ 5           N              ♡ 10 7 2
◇ A K J 10 5 4  W   E        ◇ 9
♣ Q 9 4 2        S           ♣ J 8 7 3
            ♠ J 8 3
            ♡ K J 9 8 4 3
            ◇ Q 6
            ♣ A 6
```

The contract was Four Hearts, and after winning two rounds of diamonds West switched to a spade in response to his partner's signal; East won with the queen and exited with a trump.

South knew that he had a diamond menace against West and it seemed very likely that the jack of spades was a menace against East; with clubs all round him, South could see the way to a double squeeze. An important preliminary was to play off the ace of spades, a Vienna coup. Then the trumps were led out and this end position was reached:

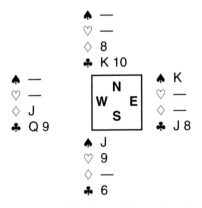

```
            ♠ —
            ♡ —
            ◇ 8
            ♣ K 10
♠ —                    ♠ K
♡ —        N          ♡ —
◇ J      W   E        ◇ —
♣ Q 9      S          ♣ J 8
            ♠ J
            ♡ 9
            ◇ —
            ♣ 6
```

The last trump wrings a club from West, the diamond is thrown from dummy and East is squeezed.

The suicide squeeze

When there are no long suits around, a double squeeze is often needed to land the ninth trick at no-trumps. The timing of such hands may present a difficulty. Declarer's play of the following hand is worth careful study.

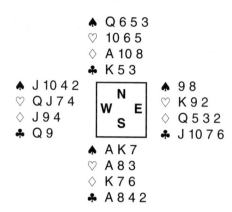

West led a low heart against Three No-Trumps; East won with the king and returned the nine. Declarer has eight tricks on top and several chances of a ninth; but if both black suits break badly a squeeze may be necessary, so the first step is to project the play to the point at which four tricks have been lost. South should not hold off the second round of hearts; he should win with the ace and return the suit at once; if West has five hearts, let him play off his winners and force his partner to make three discards.

West won the third round of hearts with the jack and played off the queen. He would have done better not to play this card; it was, in effect, the squeeze card. A club was discarded from dummy, East and South threw diamonds. West followed with a low spade, declarer won and, as he could afford to lose a trick, ducked a club. A spade came back and this was the position:

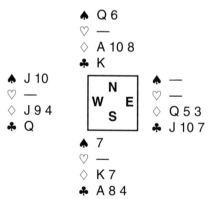

Declarer played off the king of clubs and then the queen of spades. This card began the squeeze; East had to let go a diamond and two tricks later the ace of clubs squeezed West. When he played the heart at the third trick declarer could not foresee this ending in detail; but the play was right in principle, and this is how such hands should be played.

Variations of the double squeeze

The last hand did not reduce to a three-card ending because declarer had no card with which to effect a simultaneous squeeze at the eleventh trick. The squeeze was still effective because the menaces were positioned in the most favourable way, on the left of the opponent whom they threatened. If one of the menaces is not so placed, compensation is needed in the form of an additional entry. Study this diagram:

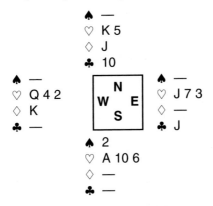

The one-card menace in clubs is in front of East instead of over him, but there is compensation in the form of an additional entry in hearts, so that the two of spades effects a double squeeze. The position is quite common.

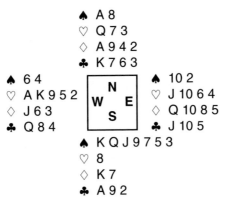

Against Six Spades West led the king of hearts and followed with a trump. There is a one-card menace against West in hearts, and if a menace can be established against East in diamonds neither opponent will be able to keep control of clubs. So declarer draws trumps and takes three rounds of diamonds, ruffing the third. This is the end position:

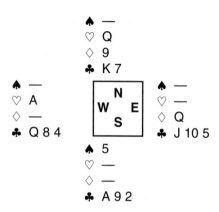

When the last trump is played, both opponents are squeezed in turn. When there is an extra high card in the suit of the double menace, the two one-card menaces can both be in the same hand. This is a familiar position:

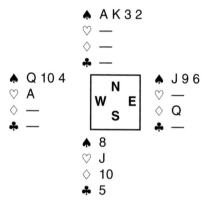

Owing to the extra control in spades there is room in the South hand for both one-card menaces and for the squeeze card.

Two tricks from a squeeze

In all the examples given up to now the squeeze has been worth one trick only. A squeeze that wins two tricks is not a double squeeze, for it operates against only one opponent; a double squeeze cannot possibly be worth two tricks. To win two extra tricks from a squeeze, declarer must have menaces against one opponent in three suits. Two one-card menaces and one two-card menace are enough only if the two-card menace is extended, as in the following diagram:

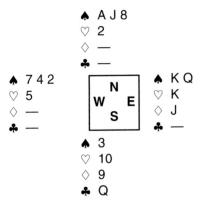

This is a repeating squeeze. Declarer leads the queen of clubs and throws the heart from dummy. East cannot afford to throw a spade and if he discards a heart or a diamond he is squeezed again. If West could control the third round of spades the squeeze would not be worth two tricks, for East could discard a spade on the first lead.

When there is no extended menace, like the spades in the diagram above, there must be a two-card menace in dummy, a two-card menace in declarer's hand, and a one-card menace on the left of the player who is to be squeezed. The smallest compass for this ending is five cards.

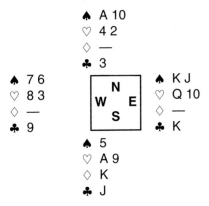

There are five cards left and South can win only three tricks by top cards. However, East has to look after three suits, and no matter how he discards on the king of diamonds he is squeezed again. The precise arrangement of menaces which makes this kind of progressive squeeze possible is not very common, but the play is important because it turns up mostly in slam contracts.

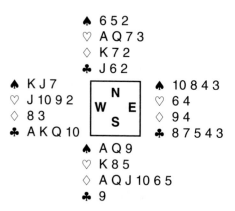

North/South reached Six Diamonds, treating with contempt a take-out double on the first round by West. Clubs were led and continued, and as the king of spades was sure to be wrong, declarer had nothing better to do than lead all the trumps and hope that if the hearts did not break they were held by West. This was the end position:

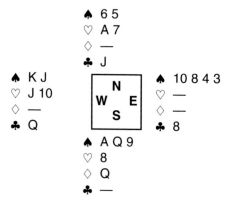

On the last trump West was squeezed in three suits, and however he plays, a second squeeze follows.

The guard squeeze

We noticed earlier in this chapter that certain variations in the arrangement of menace cards are possible when there is a compensating factor such as an additional entry. A different form of compensation arises when one opponent has to protect the other from a possible finesse. Study this diagram:

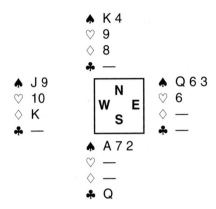

Instead of each defender controlling a one-card menace, West controls both, yet South makes all the tricks by virtue of the finesse position in spades. If West discards a spade on the queen of clubs there is a finesse against his partner's queen. This is known as a guard squeeze, because West has to keep a guard to protect his partner from a finesse. A remarkable fact about the position in the diagram is that the squeeze is successful even if East also controls one of the one-card menaces. This is a characteristic of the guard squeeze; in all other squeeze positions a one-card menace which both opponents control is of no value against best defence. To prepare for a guard squeeze it is sometimes necessary to unblock the suit in which the finesse is threatened.

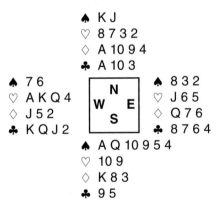

Defending Four Spades, West leads two top hearts, followed by the king of clubs. A second club is won in dummy and, taking care to unblock diamonds by discarding the nine and ten, declarer manoeuvres towards this end position:

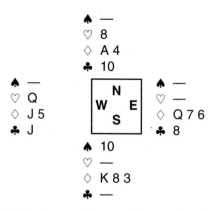

On the last spade West has to throw a diamond and South wins the last three tricks by finessing against East.

Another form of the guard squeeze is shown in this diagram:

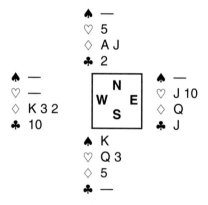

On the king of spades West throws a diamond and North a heart. East must let go a club; he cannot throw his queen of diamonds, because this protects West from a finesse. After East's club discard West is squeezed by the queen of hearts. This is a difficult and little-known form of squeeze; the sign to look for is a one-card menace which both opponents control, together with a two-card menace against East and a double menace which contains the possibility of a finesse.

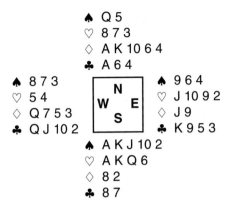

South reaches a contract of Six Spades and the queen of clubs is led. Declarer holds off this trick and a second club is won by the ace. The diamonds cannot be set up owing to lack of entries to dummy, so declarer plays off one top diamond and then leads out four trumps and two hearts. These are the last four cards:

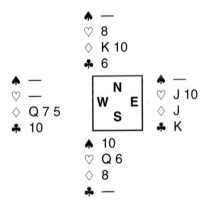

The ten of spades forces East to throw a club, and West is then squeezed on a heart lead. Note that it is a mistake to play the queen of hearts before the squeeze card.

The trump squeeze

Finally, certain squeezes are possible owing to the element of trumps. This is a typical trump squeeze:

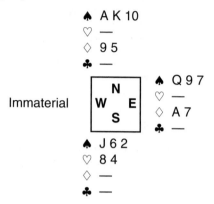

Immaterial

Hearts are trumps, and on the eight of hearts a spade is thrown from dummy; East is squeezed, for if he discards a diamond South can enter dummy and ruff out the ace. The characteristic position in a trump squeeze is that two of dummy's suits are obstructed by the right-hand opponent; dummy must hold the master card of one of these suits and a second entry as well; the second entry may lie in the suit of which dummy holds the master, as in the diagram above, or in a side suit, as in the hand which follows.

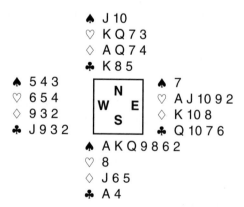

The contract was Six Spades, doubled by East on the strength of his holding in the red suits, which had been bid by dummy. A heart was led and the king fell to the ace. The queen of hearts won the second trick, and after five rounds of trumps and ace of clubs this was the position:

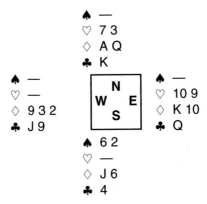

On the six of spades dummy throws the queen of diamonds and East the queen of clubs; then a club to the king forces East to unguard one of the red suits.

Summary of this chapter

It may help players to whom advanced squeeze play is a new subject if the main points made in this chapter are summarised.

Double squeeze

When there is a one-card menace against each opponent and a two-card double menace which both opponents control, a straightforward double squeeze is played.

If both menaces are placed favourably, on the left of the players whom they threaten, the play can be reduced to a three-card ending. If one of the menaces is on the wrong side, in front of the player whom it threatens, there must be some compensating factor: either an additional entry to dummy or an extension to the double menace.

There are some more complicated positions in which, instead of one double and two single menaces, two double and one two-card menace combine to effect a double squeeze.

Progressive squeeze

To be worth two tricks a squeeze must contain menaces against one opponent in three suits. There must be an extended two-card menace plus two one-card menaces, or two two-card menaces plus a one-card menace on the left of the opponent to be squeezed.

Guard squeeze

This takes place when one opponent controls two suits and has to keep a card in the third suit in order to protect his partner from a finesse. The squeeze is unique in that it succeeds even if a one-card menace is controlled by both players.

Trump squeeze

The factor of trumps makes it possible to squeeze the right-hand opponent even when there is no two-card menace in dummy. When the squeeze begins, declarer's hand contains a menace in a suit of which the master card is held by dummy, and dummy holds two plain cards in another suit of which declarer is void; if the opponent discards from this suit, a trick can be established by ruffing. In addition (because it must be possible to enter dummy twice) there must be an extra entry in dummy, either in the suit of which dummy has the top card, or in a third suit.

There are also double trump squeezes, in which both opponents need to keep cards in a suit which declarer threatens to establish by ruffing, and double guard squeezes. Some other squeeze situations, arising mostly from entry difficulties which are quite common at the table, are described in my later book, *The Expert Game*.

16

Defence to Squeeze Play

There are two sides to this: discarding correctly in an end game when the squeeze is imperfect, and preventing a perfect squeeze from developing by correct play earlier in the hand. When we speak of correct discarding, we mean more than keeping the right cards at the eleventh and twelfth trick.

To discard correctly, the first essential is to know what is going on and to have a good idea of where the cards lie. This is done by observation and inference and is something which cannot be taught. But there are some rather complicated situations in which, even if the distribution is known, the right defence is not easy to find unless certain general principles are understood. The play is always difficult when a defender has a choice of discards from two double menaces.

Discarding from two double menaces

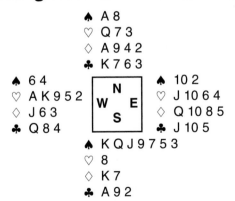

The contract was Six Spades and West led the king of hearts followed by a trump. This led to the double squeeze position shown on page 166. Now suppose that West had been so inspired as to lead a club at the second trick. This would have broken up the entries for a perfect double squeeze, but West would still have had to face some difficult discards. Declarer's best play would be to win the club in dummy and run off five trumps, leading to this position.

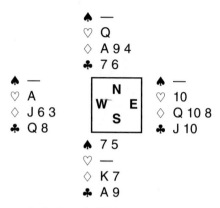

The seven of trumps is led and all West's cards are 'busy'. Obviously he cannot let go the ace of hearts. Diamonds and clubs are controlled by East as well, so the position is that there are two double menaces and West has to let go his hold on one or the other. The only defence for West is to let go a diamond; a club is thrown by dummy and a heart by East. The last trump follows and West must throw another diamond; if a diamond is thrown from dummy East must throw one as well; if dummy throws a club or a heart, East lets go a club. Declarer cannot come to the extra trick.

If in the diagram position West had thrown a club on the seven of spades, dummy would have thrown a club and East a heart. Then the ace of clubs would be cashed and the last spade would effect a simultaneous double squeeze. There is a fairly simple rule to guide the defender in a position of this kind: when there are two double menaces, the defender should unguard the suit in which the menace lies on his left.

Here is another tricky position in which the right defence would be very difficult to work out in actual play unless this rule was understood.

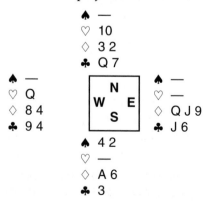

South, needing all five tricks, leads the four of spades. If West knew that his partner had a good hold in diamonds he might think that he could safely throw the four of diamonds. North and East discard a diamond and declarer follows with the last spade. If West discards a club now, his partner is squeezed on this trick; so West must throw a second diamond. A diamond is thrown from dummy and East has to throw a club; then the ace of diamonds from South squeezes West in hearts and clubs. Another line of play is for South to play the ace of diamonds after the four of spades. Then the last trump effects a simultaneous double squeeze.

Knowledge of the rule given above would have protected West from this endplay. As the diamonds were held on his right, and the clubs on his left, clubs were the suit to unguard. North and East discard diamonds and South plays his last spade. West lets go a second club and declarer has in effect to make a premature discard from dummy; if East plays correctly the defenders must win the last trick.

Protecting a double menace or a one-card menace

A deceptive position arises when a defender has to discard either from a suit in which there is a double menace or from a suit in which a one-card menace is protected by both defenders. Study this diagram:

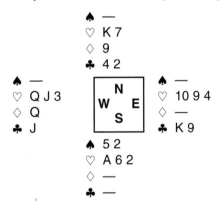

South needs all the remaining tricks and leads the five of spades. To discard a diamond is immediately fatal, so West has to choose between a heart, which both players can protect, and the jack of clubs. If he knew that his partner held the clubs West might think it was safe to unguard that suit. If West does throw the jack of clubs, then the last spade squeezes both players.

On the first lead West has to throw the three of hearts. North and East throw clubs and South plays the last spade. West discards a heart again and there is no squeeze. The discard by West of a heart in the diagram position was made in accordance with this principle: when the choice lies between unguarding a double menace or a one-card menace doubly held, the suit to unguard is the one in which the double menace is held. Another way to look at it is this: a squeeze cannot be brought off against a player who controls two one-card menaces (except when there is a guard squeeze); so in the position above West must make it his job to protect the two one-card menaces, in clubs and diamonds, while East looks after the hearts.

Defending a three-suit squeeze

It was remarked in the last chapter that the positions in which declarer can win two extra tricks by means of a squeeze against one opponent in three suits are not common. The reason for this is that such a squeeze is perfect only when there is a two-card menace in both hands and a one-card menace in the hand sitting over the defender who is being squeezed. Extra tricks are often made in play when the arrangement of menaces is not exact. This is a tricky ending for West to defend:

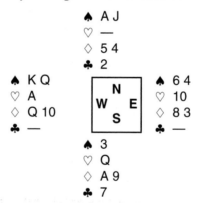

At no-trumps South leads the seven of clubs. Although there are two two-card menaces and one one-card menace, all lying against West, the squeeze for two extra tricks is not perfect, because the one-card menace is underneath West instead of over him. Whatever West discards on the seven of clubs, he must give up one trick; but so long as he discards a spade he doesn't have to give up a second trick. The principle of discarding is the same as that explained above: the discard is made in the suit which is held on the left of the player.

When there is an extension to a two-card menace a repeating squeeze can be brought off with the help of two one-card menaces. However, those one-card menaces have to be in the hand opposite the extended two-card menace; otherwise the position can be defended.

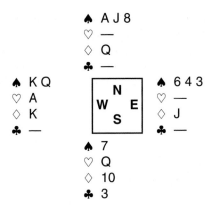

South leads three of clubs. If West discards the queen of spades dummy's spades are all good, and if West discards the ace of hearts the queen is a second squeeze card from South. The only defence is to throw the king of diamonds; then East's jack of diamonds saves the situation, for if East did not hold this card the declarer could still succeed by throwing the queen from dummy. The principle of defence here is that West discards a diamond rather than a heart in order to avoid a squeeze card being led from the hand opposite the two-card menace.

Undertrumping to avoid a squeeze

There is one rather peculiar position, not very common in actual play, in which a defender's only way of avoiding a squeeze is to 'discard' a trump.

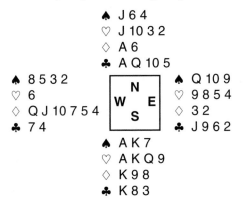

The contract is Seven Hearts and West leads the queen of diamonds. Declarer wins in dummy, takes a round of trumps and then plays the king and another diamond, ruffing with the jack. It is not difficult to see that if East discards either a spade or a club he presents declarer with his thirteenth trick. So it is natural to underruff instead of discarding from one of the black suits. You would think that this was only postponing the evil day, but as it turns out, the squeeze in spades and hearts never comes off. The reason is that both menaces, the fourth club and the jack of spades, are protected by the player who sits over them. So when South plays his squeeze card, the last heart, dummy is squeezed in front of East.

Tactical defence

Up to now we have considered only how imperfect squeezes can be prevented by correct discarding. The rest of the chapter shows how a perfect squeeze can be prevented by correct tactics earlier in the play. We found in Chapter 13 that a successful squeeze depends upon various factors such as menaces, entries and timing. These three are all open to assault by the defenders. First of all, menaces.

The assault on menace cards

One way to prevent declarer from establishing the menace cards which he needs is to protect partner's hand when partner is in danger of being squeezed. This is a matter of correct discarding, which we have already looked at. In the last hand, for example, on page 179, it is imperative for West to hold on to the eight of spades in order to control the third round of the suit; for if West throws spades early in the hand, South's seven becomes a menace against East. The second way to prevent declarer from developing menace cards is to upset the entries which he needs to establish them. In the following hand West has only to refrain from actively assisting declarer to isolate the menace.

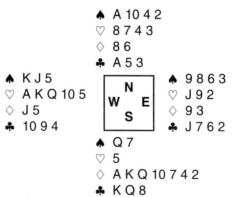

The contract is Six Diamonds and West leads the king of hearts, on which East plays the two. West may be sure that declarer has a singleton heart, so nothing is gained by continuing the suit. In fact, it is fatal to lead another round of hearts, for that gives South the chance to ruff out a third round of the suit and so establish the last heart as a one-card menace lying exclusively against West. Then after all the trumps and clubs have been played, West will be squeezed in spades and hearts on the eleventh trick. West should foresee this danger and should lead a diamond or club to the second trick. Then East can hold on to his jack of hearts and West can let go all his hearts and so avoid the squeeze.

The hand just given makes an interesting comparison with the one that follows; this time West extinguishes the menace by leading the suit in which the menace lies.

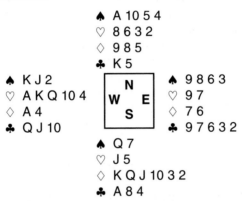

The contract is Four Diamonds and West leads the king of hearts, followed by the ace. Now another round of hearts is essential; West comes in again with the ace of diamonds and plays a fourth round to kill dummy's menace. Then there is no squeeze and declarer has to lose a spade in addition to two hearts and a diamond.

The attack on entries

The defenders have more chance to kill entries than they have to kill menaces. It is very easy to be careless on such a hand as the following:

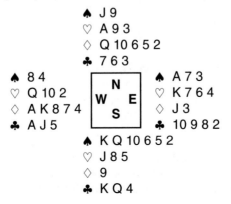

After West had opened with One Diamond, South became declarer in Two Spades. The king of diamonds was led and at the second trick West tried a low heart, won by East's king. A club return looked best and the king lost to the ace; West led back the jack, declarer won and led trumps. East let dummy win the first spade and won the second round with the ace. The position was:

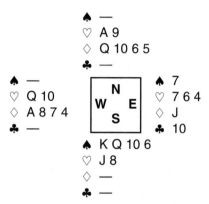

```
              ♠ —
              ♡ A 9
              ◊ Q 10 6 5
              ♣ —
  ♠ —                        ♠ 7
  ♡ Q 10        N            ♡ 7 6 4
  ◊ A 8 7 4   W   E          ◊ J
  ♣ —            S           ♣ 10
              ♠ K Q 10 6
              ♡ J 8
              ◊ —
              ♣ —
```

Either a diamond or a club return looked harmless, and in practice East led a club. Declarer ruffed and ran off the spades, squeezing West in hearts and diamonds. Of course, East should have foreseen the danger and should have led a heart to break up the entries. This sort of position is extremely common in play.

The next hand looks like a problem, but the right defence was found in actual play.

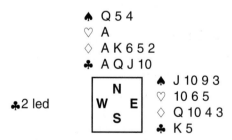

```
              ♠ Q 5 4
              ♡ A
              ◊ A K 6 5 2
              ♣ A Q J 10
                              ♠ J 10 9 3
                   N          ♡ 10 6 5
  ♣2 led       W       E      ◊ Q 10 4 3
                   S          ♣ K 5
```

The contract was Six No-Trumps by South, who had bid first hearts and then spades. The two of clubs was led and the queen was finessed. The problem is, what should East play to the second trick? South bid hearts before spades, so was likely to hold at least five hearts and four spades, together with three clubs if partner's lead of the two was a true card.

It was probable, therefore, that South had only a singleton diamond. If South held A-K-x-x in spades and K-Q-x-x-x in hearts, then there were eleven tricks on top and the twelfth would come from a double squeeze.

At the finish South would have a spade, a heart and a diamond in his own hand, and A-K-6 of diamonds in dummy; at that point neither defender would be able to hold three diamonds. This position could be prevented if the entry to dummy were killed at once. So to the second trick East returned the queen of diamonds – the queen because South's singleton might be the jack. This play was the only defence to beat the hand, for South held:

♠ A K 6 2
♡ K Q 9 7 3
◇ J
♣ 7 6 3

The assault on timing

The most difficult defence of all is that which interferes with declarer's timing. When we discussed the submarine squeeze we saw that declarer has often to lose a critical trick early on in order to bring off his squeeze. Sometimes it happens that the defenders can avoid winning a critical trick and so spoil the timing for the squeeze. We have already seen, on page 164, an example of the suicide squeeze. It is a stratagem on the declarer's part in which he gives an opponent a chance to lead out winners which have the effect of squeezing the other defender. This is a fairly simple example:

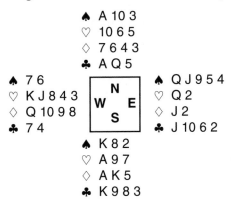

```
              ♠ A 10 3
              ♡ 10 6 5
              ◇ 7 6 4 3
              ♣ A Q 5
  ♠ 7 6                      ♠ Q J 9 5 4
  ♡ K J 8 4 3      N         ♡ Q 2
  ◇ Q 10 9 8    W   E        ◇ J 2
  ♣ 7 4            S         ♣ J 10 6 2
              ♠ K 8 2
              ♡ A 9 7
              ◇ A K 5
              ♣ K 9 8 3
```

West leads a heart against Three No-Trumps, East wins with the queen and returns a heart. It is good play for South to win with the ace and lead a heart himself. South has eight tricks on top and a very good chance of coming to the ninth if he can induce West to play off his hearts. If West has only a four-card suit, then no harm is done; if the suit is 5-2, West should be given a chance to make his tricks. It is easy to see that if West plays off all his hearts he very much embarrasses his partner. East lets go two spades and one diamond, but when declarer subsequently plays the two top diamonds East is squeezed in the black suits. The right defence is for

West to make only one of his long hearts; then he switches to spades in response to the high-low signal made by partner on the last two tricks, and declarer has no way of forcing the ninth trick.

These situations are, of course, difficult to judge in play; often one cannot tell whether or not to cash a winner. In general, this is a fair rule to remember: be wary of playing off a winner which completes the 'bag' for your side; if the contract is Three No-Trumps, don't be in too much of a hurry to win your fourth trick unless you have a good idea where the fifth is coming from. For some reason players are more concerned to protect their partners than they are to protect themselves. So, many players who wouldn't fall into the trap on the last hand would go wrong on the next.

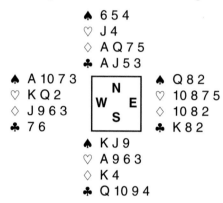

♠ 6 5 4
♡ J 4
◇ A Q 7 5
♣ A J 5 3

♠ A 10 7 3   ♠ Q 8 2
♡ K Q 2   ♡ 10 8 7 5
◇ J 9 6 3   ◇ 10 8 2
♣ 7 6   ♣ K 8 2

♠ K J 9
♡ A 9 6 3
◇ K 4
♣ Q 10 9 4

West leads a small spade against Three No-Trumps and declarer wins with the king. The club finesse loses and East plays a spade; West wins with the ten and plays off the ace. If at this point West plays off the thirteenth spade he is in difficulties when the third and fourth rounds of clubs are played; he can discard a heart on the third club, but the fourth club is fatal. West should foresee this position and should refrain from playing off the thirteenth spade, for that card has the effect of 'rectifying the count' for declarer. Instead of playing off the seven of spades West should play back a harmless club. On the third round of clubs he discards a heart, and the position is:

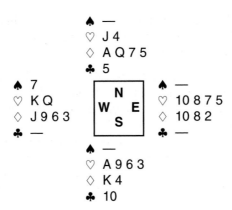

When the last club is played, West discards his spade and declarer is left without resource.